THE CLINTONS

THEIR STORY IN PHOTOGRAPHS

Created by David Elliot Cohen

Foreword by Chris Matthews

STERLING
New York

STERLING
New York

An Imprint of Sterling Publishing
387 Park Avenue South
New York, NY 10016

ISBN 978-1-4027-8788-1

Distributed in Canada by Sterling Publishing
c/o Canadian Manda Group, 165 Dufferin Street
Toronto, Ontario, Canada M6K 3H6
Distributed in the United Kingdom by GMC Distribution Services
Castle Place, 166 High Street, Lewes, East Sussex, England BN7 1XU
Distributed in Australia by Capricorn Link (Australia) Pty. Ltd.
P.O. Box 704, Windsor, NSW 2756, Australia

Please see pages 222–224 for text and picture credits.

For information about custom editions, special sales, and premium and corporate purchases, please contact Sterling Special Sales at 800-805-5489 or specialsales@sterlingpublishing.com.

Manufactured in China

2 4 6 8 10 9 7 5 3 1

www.sterlingpublishing.com

FATHERLESS CHILD: Virginia Cassidy Blythe, in the autumn of 1946, holds her son, William Jefferson Blythe III—later two-term US president Bill Clinton. Bill's father, the first of Virginia's four husbands, died in an automobile accident three months before the future chief executive was born.

FOREWORD

By Chris Matthews

Author of *Jack Kennedy: Elusive Hero* and host of MSNBC's *Hardball*

Bill and Hillary Clinton stand today as the great couple of our generation.

I'm speaking of the Sixties. These two remarkable people have carried forward that era, with all its zest and disturbance, through a half century of human drama and historic achievement.

Just look at them! Their very faces carry the iconic memory of their times. The turmoil of Vietnam and civil rights, and even the sexual revolution, all left an enduring imprint on them.

You can see the turmoil of the campus in them still. To be a college student in the true Sixties—that cultural decade between Dallas and Nixon's resignation—was to face a choice between rebel and defender—or, in the argot of the times, "straight-arrow" and "freak."

Was it a sign of weakness or strength in their characters that neither Bill nor Hillary made the choice? They insisted on marrying the ambitions rooted in their childhoods with the zeitgeist of their college years. They were affected by the campus but not diverted. They rejected the dictates of their peers just as they rejected the limits imposed on their parents.

Look at young Bill with his 1950s ambitions for student council office, his aim for law school and a political career, his eager reach for that handshake with President Kennedy. Watch him cover it with those sideburns, long hair, and 1960s swagger. No, he never "inhaled" anything that would get between him and what he would one day call his political viability.

Look at young Hillary Rodham. A Goldwater Girl who had read *The Conscience of a Conservative*, she chose the all-female Wellesley College. There she turned left, attracted to the cerebral Eugene McCarthy's anti-war campaign. It was a natural pivot from libertarian to a liberal suspicion of the imperial presidency of Lyndon Johnson. (I know because I shared it.)

How natural that these two brains should meet and love what they met. How true a marriage, built as it would be on their shared natures. Both of them were a hybrid of ambition and idealism, of the inherited desire for personal achievement and recognition.

The beauty of the pictures in this book is the unifying story they tell about the Clintons.

Like the Sixties, which would forever shape it, their story is not of unrelenting success. No fan can tell their story without accounting for the falls. No critic can tell it without admitting the recoveries. No historian can narrate this joint biography without confessing that the rises outmatch the falls. Again and again, a loss of footing on the climb somehow landed each of them, often together, on a yet higher cliff.

Call it luck only at your peril. My strongest, best memory of Bill Clinton was of him standing in a college gym up in New Hampshire. It was the last weekend before the 1992 primary. He'd been shelled by a woman's charges of a long-ago affair, and buffeted just that week by the notorious "draft letter" that showed him avoiding Vietnam-era military service. And yet there he was, standing in that gym with crowds on every side of him, answering every question they could throw at him.

I remember my friend Hendrik Hertzberg, now of *The New Yorker*, saying he could not imagine anyone of our generation doing what Clinton was doing. We were sitting in the stands as Clinton stood before us taking the heat for what he'd done.

Good for him, I say, not for what he'd done but for his readiness to stand up to the hypocrisy being thrown at him. He was willing to weather the assault that comes laserlike at those who, with all their faults, dare to stand up and say, "Choose me."

Again and again, Bill Clinton has done this. Beaten for student council president at Georgetown, he won a Rhodes Scholarship. Beaten for Congress, he ran for and won election as attorney general and then governor of Arkansas. Beaten for reelection, he came back and won the office four times in a row. Beaten in that 1992 New Hampshire primary, he came back and won the presidency. When his party lost control of Congress in 1994, he scrambled his staff, adjusted politically, and won reelection handily. Impeached in 1998, he ended his second term with overwhelming public approval.

His accomplishments at home include NAFTA, the Brady Bill, the Family and Medical Leave Act, COBRA, welfare reform, and four years of balanced budgets. Overseas he led the way to the Oslo Accords on the Mideast, the Dayton Accords on the Balkans, and my favorite, the Belfast Agreement on Northern Ireland.

Hillary has proven his match. As first lady, US senator from New York, and secretary of state, she has already made history at the highest level. She has broken ground as no woman has before her. As I write this, there is no way to know how far she will go.

Today, the Clintons are figures admired around the globe. To travel with them is to feel the admiration all hopeful people feel toward those who dare, given all they are, and all they aren't, to lead us to a better world.

Washington, DC
February 2012

THE FATHER HE NEVER KNEW: Bill Clinton's biological father, Bill Blythe Jr., was one of nine children born to poor farmers in Sherman, Texas. Blythe married his first wife, Virginia Gash, when he was seventeen. They divorced thirteen months later, but subsequently conceived a son named Henry—the oldest of Bill Clinton's three half-siblings. In 1940, Blythe married his first wife's sister, Minnie Faye. The marriage was annulled after four months— just before Blythe, a traveling salesman, married Wanetta Alexander of Kansas City—already pregnant with Blythe's daughter, Sharon Lee. Blythe divorced Wanetta in April 1944, seven months after his bigamous fourth marriage to Virginia Cassidy of Hope, Arkansas. Virginia gave birth to William Jefferson Blythe III—later Bill Clinton—on August 19, 1946, three months after the twenty-eight-year-old Blythe died in a Missouri auto accident. Virginia would not discover her husband's three previous marriages—nor would Bill learn of his two older stepsiblings—until they were publicly revealed in a *Washington Post* article published on Father's Day, 1993.

AN UNLIKELY FUTURE: An early 1947 portrait of William Jefferson Blythe III, not yet one year old, taken in Hope, Arkansas—a segregated railroad town of 7,500 people founded in 1875. Born poor, the son of a young widowed mother, raised by loving grandparents until he was nearly four, Billy Blythe would change his name to Bill Clinton when he was sixteen, then go on to become a Phi Beta Kappa graduate of Georgetown University, a Rhodes Scholar at Oxford, a Yale Law School graduate, America's youngest governor in five decades, and eventually the first two-term Democratic president since the patrician Franklin Delano Roosevelt five decades earlier.

HIS ONLY PHOTO: Virginia Cassidy Blythe, twenty-three, with Bill Blythe Jr. at Chicago's ritzy Palmer House Hotel in 1946. In 1943, Bill and Virginia were married in Shreveport, Louisiana, where Virginia was training to be a nurse. Shortly after the ceremony, Bill shipped out for combat duty in Italy. When World War II ended, the Blythes moved to Chicago, where Bill resumed his pre-war job selling machine parts for the Manbee Equipment Company. Bill and Virginia bought a house in suburban Forest Park, Illinois—coincidentally, about ten miles from the childhood home of Hillary Rodham.

Since Virginia Blythe was pregnant, and the couple couldn't move into their new house right away, she decided to spend time with her parents in Hope, Arkansas. Bill Blythe was driving south from Chicago to pick her up when he was killed in an automobile accident. Bill Clinton later wrote that this was his only photo of his mother and father together. Although they never met, William Jefferson Blythe Jr. made an indelible impression on the future president. "[He] left me with the feeling that I had to live for two people," Bill later wrote, "and that if I did well enough, somehow I could make up for the life he should have had."

ARKANSAS COWBOY: Billy, in full cowboy garb, mounts a pony for a Mother's Day portrait snapped in 1949. Throughout his life, Bill's mother, Virginia, was his guiding spirit. Clinton's boundless charm and wandering eye may have come from his biological father, but his warmth, compassion, and immense "I feel your pain" empathy flowed from his vivacious, larger-than-life mother, who often told him that he would someday be president. "Every memory I have of Virginia from growing up," says Bill's childhood friend, Joe Purvis, "she was smiling."

STEPDAD: In 1952, Billy's mother, Virginia Blythe, returned from New Orleans, where she had trained for two years as a nurse-anesthetist. She retrieved Bill from his loving grandparents, Edith and Jim Cassidy, who raised him during her absence. Then Virginia married her longtime beau—the charming, generous, and hard-drinking Roger Clinton, nicknamed Dude—who owned the local Buick dealership and moonlighted as a bouncer. Virginia's parents took a dim view of the union—appropriately, it turned out—and would not attend the wedding. After the nuptials, Roger, Virginia, and Billy moved eighty miles north to Roger's hometown of Hot Springs—at the time, an illegal gambling mecca known as the "Sin City" of Arkansas.

BABY STEPS: Hillary Diane Rodham, probably in Park Ridge, Illinois, circa 1950, when the future first lady, New York senator, presidential candidate, and US secretary of state was two and a half years old.

Hillary's father, Hugh Rodham, was the son of British immigrants and the owner of a small textile business. During World War II, he was the naval equivalent of a drill sergeant. A surly, physically imposing, verbally abusive disciplinarian, Hugh was also a stalwart Republican who despised labor unions, "government giveaways," and high taxes.

Hillary's mother, Dorothy, was more or less abandoned by her young parents and raised by resentful grandparents in California. She would overcome her Dickensian childhood and contemptuous husband to become an intellectually curious free spirit and closet Democrat who read at the local library, taught Methodist Sunday School, and attended college in her sixties. Despite their very different personalities and divergent politics, Hillary's parents agreed on one point: with education, ambition, and hard work, Hillary and her two younger brothers would be able to accomplish anything.

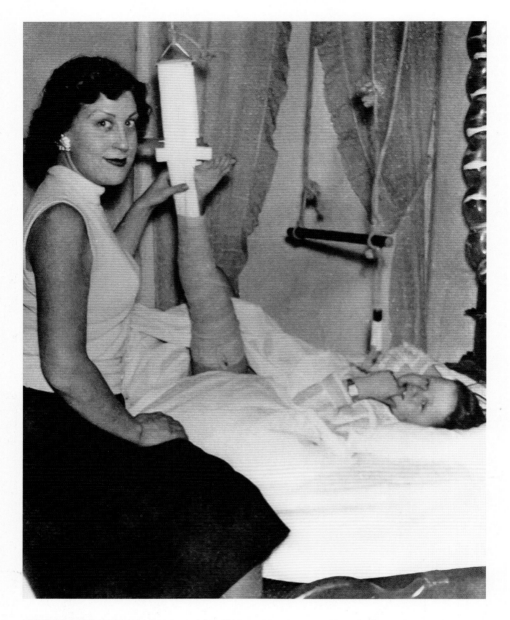

HOPALONG BILL: Five-year-old Billy Blythe recuperates at home with his mother, Virginia, a registered nurse. Billy broke his leg jumping over a rope strung across the playground of Miss Marie Purkins's School for Little Folks in Hope, Arkansas. "It wasn't even a moving rope," Bill later wrote. "All the other kids cleared it." One of Bill's kindergarten classmates, Thomas F. "Mack" McLarty III, would later become an all-state high school quarterback, a summa cum laude graduate of the University of Arkansas, an Arkansas state legislator, CEO of a Fortune 500 company, and, eventually, President Clinton's first White House chief of staff.

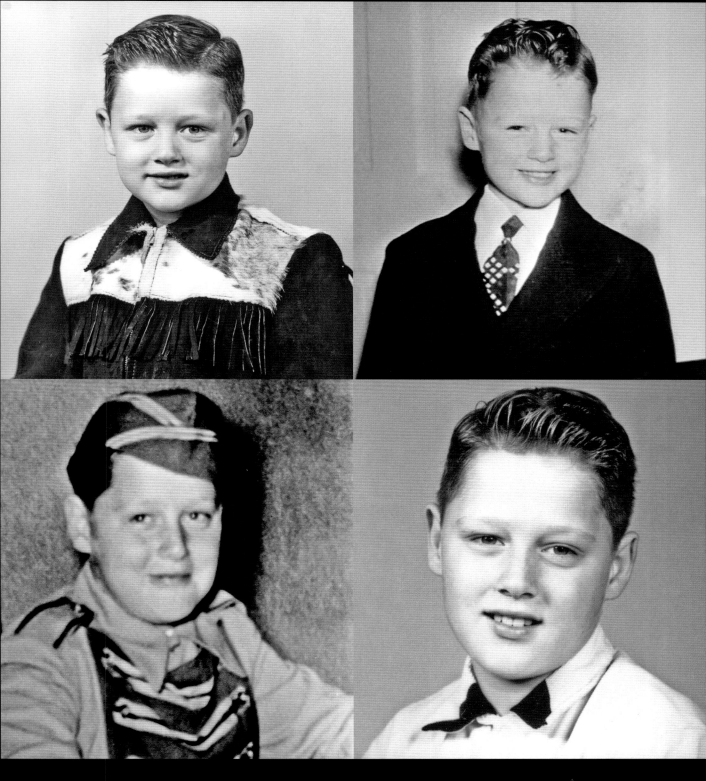

BOYHOOD PORTRAITS: Clockwise from upper left, Billy Blythe, age five, in western wear in 1952; dressed for church, circa 1953; a fifth-grade school photo from Ramble Elementary School in Hot Springs, Arkansas; Bill in his band uniform, circa 1956–57.

A GIFTED MUSICIAN: Bill holds a tenor saxophone on his twelfth birthday—August 19, 1958—at home in Hot Springs, Arkansas. The future president loved the gospel music he heard most Sundays at Park Place Baptist Church. He won first chair in the Arkansas state band's saxophone section and once considered a musical career. "I loved music and thought I could be very good," Clinton later wrote in his autobiography. "But I knew I would never be John Coltrane or Stan Getz." Clinton would, however, use his saxophone skills to further his political career. In 1992, the presidential candidate appeared on the popular *Arsenio Hall Show* and belted out Elvis Presley's "Heartbreak Hotel" with the band. It may have been coincidence, but shortly after his performance, Clinton took his first lead in the presidential polls.

HALF-BROTHER: Bill, thirteen, with mother Virginia and three-year-old half-brother Roger Clinton Jr. in 1959. When Roger was born, Virginia's husband was drinking heavily. "I think she, and probably he too, thought [Roger's birth] might save their marriage," Clinton later wrote, but "instead of making him happy and responsible, the birth of his only son prompted him to run back to the bottle." Even before they married, Roger physically abused Virginia, and his drunken rages worsened over time. Roger once pulled a gun and shot the wall above Virginia's head, and he occasionally beat her. That ended when Bill grew large enough to intervene—the first time at age fifteen with a golf club in his hand. Roger's alcoholism and abuse would have a deeply negative effect on Roger Jr.

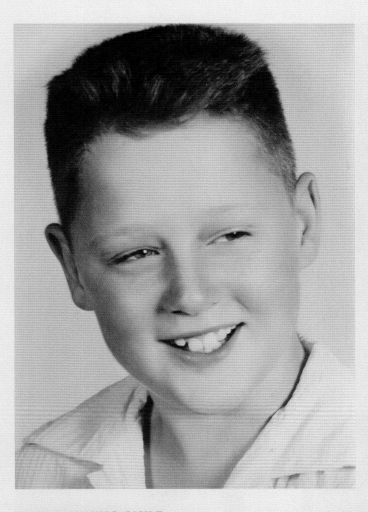

THAT WINNING SMILE: Despite his abusive household, Billy Blythe maintained a sunny, optimistic disposition. He learned to keep his stepfather's violent, alcohol-fueled episodes secret—even from close friends—and he remained ever hopeful that his family life would improve. In 1962, when Virginia divorced Roger and then reconciled with him three months later, Bill tried to curry favor with his stepfather by legally changing his name from William Jefferson Blythe III to William Jefferson Clinton. Virginia later said that "if [Roger] ever loved anything in this world it was Bill," but Bill's stepfather never offered to adopt him.

YOUNG REPUBLICAN: Hillary Rodham was obsessed with politics from an early age, avidly debating the issues of the day with her classmates and usually taking the more conservative position. In a nod to her Republican father and her conservative ninth-grade history teacher, Hillary read Arizona senator Barry Goldwater's influential 123-page manifesto, *The Conscience of a Conservative,* and became a "Goldwater Girl" during the 1964 presidential campaign. "I was an active Young Republican right down to my cowgirl outfit and straw cowboy hat emblazoned with the slogan 'AuH$_2$O' [the chemical symbols for gold and water]," Hillary later wrote. Despite the socially conscious influence of her young Methodist minister, Donald Jones—who took her to hear Dr. Martin Luther King Jr. speak in nearby Chicago—Hillary's political philosophy would not shift leftward until she attended elite Wellesley College.

35, MEET 42: The future forty-second president of the United States meets the thirty-fifth chief executive, John F. Kennedy, in the White House Rose Garden on July 26, 1963—four months before Kennedy's assassination. Clinton, sixteen at the time, was one of Arkansas's two representatives—called "senators"—to the American Legion Boys Nation summer program at the University of Maryland. One hundred Boys Nation senators from around the country toured the capital, met their congressional representatives, and then headed to the White House to meet Kennedy. Bill, one of the bigger boys, muscled his way to the front of the pack, where he would be sure to shake hands with the president.

When Clinton stumped for his own presidency nearly three decades later, this photograph—often cited as the genesis moment when Bill Clinton's presidential ambitions emerged—was used to good effect by his campaign. Other boys present that day say that Bill immediately announced his own presidential ambitions to the group. Clinton claims that—at the time, at least—he was more interested in becoming a US senator from Arkansas.

Photograph by Arnie Sachs

STUDENT POLITICIAN: Hillary Rodham, sixteen, poses for a 1964 yearbook photo with classmates at Maine East High School, where she was elected to the student council and became junior class vice president. The following year, when her suburban school district expanded its facilities to accommodate the baby boom, Hillary transferred to brand-new Maine Township High School South. There, she ran for student body president against several boys and lost. One boy told her that she was "stupid if she thought a girl could be elected president." But the boy who won the election promptly asked Hillary to head the Organizations Committee, which, Hillary later noted, did most of the actual work.

My father said he wouldn't pay for college if I went west of the Mississippi or to Radcliffe, which he heard was full of beatniks.

—Hillary Rodham Clinton,
Living History, 2003

THE GRADUATES: Like his future wife, Bill Clinton was a student politician. He was president of his junior class at segregated Hot Springs High School—a top Arkansas public school that emphasized public service. In his senior year, Bill became the school drum major, which rendered him ineligible to run for either senior class president or student council president. Instead, he ran for class secretary and was handily defeated by his next-door neighbor and close friend, Carolyn Yeldell. Clinton later noted that the election taught him never to run for an office he didn't really want.

Inspired by his Boys Nation trip to the nation's capital the previous year, Bill applied to only one college: Washington's competitive Georgetown University. Clinton, who ranked fourth in his class of 327, felt confident about his prospects—particularly when he learned that Georgetown tried to admit at least one applicant from every state—even Arkansas. But when his April 1964 acceptance letter made no mention of a scholarship, Bill had second thoughts about the cost—and about leaving Virginia and Roger Jr. behind in an abusive household without his protection. Bill's high school counselor, Edith Irons, argued that Georgetown would open important opportunities for Bill, and she prevailed.

When Hillary was a senior at Maine South in Park Ridge, Illinois, she "had no clue" where she wanted to go to college. Her guidance counselor suggested a few Midwest colleges where most local graduates matriculated, but two Northwestern University graduate students who taught government classes at her high school saw Hillary's potential and steered her toward their own alma maters—Smith and Wellesley, both elite Eastern women's colleges. Hillary attended Chicago-area events for both schools and "felt out of place." But she eventually picked Wellesley, based on a brochure photograph of a small on-campus lake. It reminded her of Lake Winola in Pennsylvania's Pocono Mountains, where she had spent many happy summers at her grandfather's cabin.

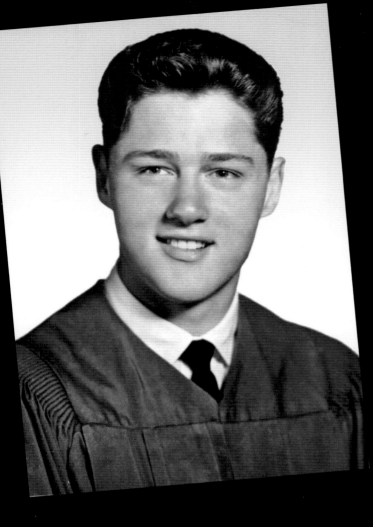

I had never seen the Georgetown campus... but I wanted to go to Washington.

— BILL CLINTON, *My Life,* 2004

COLLEGE STAR: At Georgetown—an elite Jesuit institution largely attended by well-heeled students from big-city Catholic high schools—a backwoods Baptist such as Bill Clinton was initially an outsider. But Clinton's immense energy, dashing good looks, and powerful charisma eventually won over his classmates. The foreign service major ran for, and won, the presidency of both his freshman and sophomore classes.

In his junior year, Bill sought the top job—president of the student council. His earlier success and natural optimism convinced Clinton he would win. But he failed to account for the seismic shift in student-administration relations that was sweeping America's campuses at the time—even at conservative Georgetown. Clinton's opponent, sophomore class vice president Terry Modglin, cast Bill as a glad-handing "establishment candidate," eager to appease Georgetown's Jesuit administration. A self-styled rebel, Modglin won in a landslide, and Clinton learned a hard lesson about the need to gauge the mood of the electorate.

That same year, 1967, Bill landed a prestigious clerkship with the Senate Foreign Relations Committee, then headed by the brilliant, powerful Arkansas senator J. William Fulbright—a sharp critic of America's war in Vietnam. Clinton soon shared Fulbright's belief that the United States lacked any compelling moral or strategic reason to continue its costly Vietnam adventure.

Top: Bill and Roger Clinton with their dog, King, in front of their house on Park Avenue in Hot Springs, Arkansas, on Easter Sunday, 1962. **Bottom:** Clinton's 1967 Georgetown campaign poster. **Facing page:** Clinton at Georgetown.

A REALISTIC APPROACH TO STUDENT GOVERNMENT

BILL CLINTON

CANDIDATE

PRESIDENT OF THE STUDENT COUNCIL

MAR. 8 1967

To Hillary Rodham
with best wishes
Gerald R. Ford

Hillary — you
were great —
Princess — the
spirit of
your beauty
and especially
your great work
at the 1968
Convention.
Good luck,
Mel Laird

I sometimes think that I didn't leave the Republican Party as much as it left me.

—HILLARY RODHAM CLINTON, *Living History,* 2003

REPUBLICAN INTERNSHIP: Hillary Rodham grew up as a conservative Goldwater Republican like her father, and she was still a socially liberal Rockefeller Republican when she entered Wellesley College. President of the Wellesley Young Republicans her freshman year, Hillary gradually came to the conclusion that the GOP was on the wrong side of the contentious issues that roiled America at the time: civil rights and the Vietnam War.

Hillary's political science professor, Alan Schechter, who headed the Wellesley in Washington internship program, wanted to put Hillary's leftward drift to the test, so in the summer of 1968 he assigned her to the House Republican Conference. Hillary personally liked the Republican leadership, including future president Gerald Ford, **center**; Nixon's future defense secretary Melvin Laird, **second from right**; and New York representative—later senator—Charles Goodell, **far right**. But when Goodell took Hillary to the 1968 Republican Convention to work on Nelson Rockefeller's late-entry nomination bid, Hillary was unsettled by what she perceived as "veiled racism" on the part of some convention delegates.

From that point forward, Hillary Rodham was a Democrat who supported the 1968 presidential bid of liberal, anti-war senator Eugene McCarthy. Hillary's dyed-in-the-wool Republican father, Hugh Rodham, eventually reconciled himself to his daughter's party affiliation, but when Hugh died in 1993, Hillary found this photo of herself with the Republican leadership hanging on his bedroom wall.

STUDENT LEADER: In 1968, Hillary Rodham, **top photo, center, in glasses**, was elected president of the Wellesley College Government Association. Hillary organized a student strike to protest Martin Luther King's assassination, but she also deftly facilitated communication between Wellesley students and their administration during turbulent times. Working within the system, she helped Wellesley avert the type of anarchy that fractured other college campuses. Hillary's 1969 commencement address—the first delivered by a student in Wellesley's ninety-one-year history—received a standing ovation and national attention. **Bottom**, Hillary stands with, **l–r**, Wellesley board chairman John Quarles, president Ruth Adams, and Republican senator Edward Brooke, whom Hillary reproached in her speech.

ARKANSAS TO OXFORD: While at Georgetown, Bill Clinton won a prestigious Rhodes Scholarship that paid his way to University College, Oxford, where he studied philosophy, politics, and economics. At Oxford, Clinton participated in anti–Vietnam War protests. He also used connections with his former boss, Senator William Fulbright, and Arkansas Governor Winthrop Rockefeller, to join the University of Arkansas Law School's Reserve Officer Training Corps—effectively deferring his draft and a possible deployment to Vietnam. Bill's deft manipulation of the system—he never actually attended the University of Arkansas Law School—and his subsequent letter to the Arkansas ROTC director thanking him for "saving me from the draft," would plague Clinton two decades later when he ran for president.

Photograph by Matthew Polak (bottom)

VOICE OF HER GENERATION: When the section of her rambling 1969 Wellesley commencement address that criticized Massachusetts Senator Edward Brooke was printed in *Life* magazine, Hillary Rodham became a nationally recognized spokesperson for her generation. *Life* photographed her in wild youth garb, **above** and **facing page, top left**; she appeared on a nationally syndicated television program; and she was quoted in newspapers in New England and her home state of Illinois. By the time she entered Yale Law School, she was a minor celebrity. "Hillary Rodham was a star," remembers author, film critic, and law school classmate Michael Medved. "Everyone knew about her speech and talked in reverential tones about the extraordinary wisdom and eloquence that her address had displayed."

Photographs by Lee Balterman (facing page, top left, and above)

WHEN BILL MET HILL: "Bill Clinton was hard to miss in the autumn of 1970," Hillary later wrote. "He arrived at Yale Law School looking more like a Viking than a Rhodes Scholar returning from two years at Oxford."

Robert Reich, Bill Clinton's future labor secretary, claims he introduced Bill and Hillary on the first day of class in 1969, but he recalls that neither showed much interest in the other. That would change. When they next spoke—in the Yale law library in spring, 1971—Hillary walked up to the future president and said, "If you're going to keep looking at me and I'm going to keep looking back, we at least ought to know each other. I'm Hillary Rodham."

According to Hillary, they didn't speak again until the last day of classes, when Hillary told Bill that she was going to the registrar's office to sign up for next semester's classes. Bill pretended he hadn't registered yet so he could walk with her. He then talked her into going to a Mark Rothko exhibit at the Yale University Art Gallery, only to find that the museum was closed by a labor dispute. Hillary was duly impressed when Bill talked their way in. That weekend Hillary caught a cold, and Bill brought her chicken soup and orange juice. After that, they were inseparable. Bill tagged along when Hillary traveled west to Oakland in the summer of 1971 to work at Treuhaft, Walker, and Bernstein, which handled cases involving civil rights, free speech, and the draft. When they returned to New Haven in the fall, they moved into a $75-a-month apartment together.

"He was the first man I met who was not afraid of me," Hillary later wrote.

"She conveyed a sense of strength and self-possession I had rarely seen in anyone, man or woman," recalls Bill.

POWER COUPLE: The publicity surrounding Hillary Rodham's Wellesley commencement speech opened lots of doors, including an invitation to address the League of Women Voters' fiftieth-anniversary convention. There, in May 1970, Hillary met one of her important early mentors, Marian Wright Edelman. A civil rights activist and the first African American woman admitted to the Mississippi bar, Edelman was a Yale Law School alumna and head of the Washington Research Project, a DC-based public interest law firm. Edelman, who would soon create the Children's Defense Fund, inspired Hillary to focus on children's issues. In conjunction with the Yale Child Study Center and New Haven Legal Services, Hillary developed legal protocols for abused children. Working with Edelman's Washington Research Project, she also did important research into the condition of migrant farmworkers and their families for a Senate investigation headed by Minnesota senator and future vice president Walter Mondale.

Meanwhile, Bill focused on Connecticut politics. He barely attended classes while working full-time on liberal anti-war candidate Joseph Duffey's 1970 Senate campaign. Duffey finished second in a three-way race against incumbent Thomas Dodd and the winner, Republican Lowell Weicker, but Bill came away with a store of practical experience and valuable political contacts. Together, Bill and Hillary teamed up for the 1972 mock trial competition at Yale Law School. They didn't win, but observers noted their effective teamwork and complementary styles. Classmate Nancy Bekavac, future president of Scripps College, remembered that "Hillary was very sharp and Chicago, and Bill was very *To Kill a Mockingbird.*"

POLITICO: Bill Clinton and Arkansas Democratic Party chairman Joe Purcell meet South Dakota Senator George McGovern, **center**, at Little Rock National Airport. In 1972, while still attending Yale Law School, Bill helped manage McGovern's presidential campaign in Texas. Hillary followed Bill to Austin, where she headed the Democrats' voter registration drive. McGovern won the Democratic nomination, but when his running mate, Missouri Senator Thomas Eagleton, admitted receiving electroshock therapy for depression, McGovern bungled Eagleton's exit. Republican incumbents Richard Nixon and Spiro Agnew trounced McGovern and Kennedy in-law Sargent Shriver by the largest margin in American history, winning not only Texas but also every other state in the Union except Massachusetts.

After McGovern's massive defeat, Bill and Hillary returned to Yale. When they graduated in 1973, Bill took Hillary to England. At twilight, on the shores of Ennerdale Water in England's Lake Country, Bill proposed. Hillary declined, but kept the door open by agreeing to take both the Arkansas and District of Columbia bar exams. "I realize [now] how scared I was of commitment in general and of Bill's intensity in particular," Hillary later wrote. "I thought of him as a force of nature and wondered whether I'd be up to the task of living though his seasons."

PROFESSOR CLINTON: Bill Clinton returned to Arkansas to run for public office, but he needed an income and a base of operations, so he accepted a position teaching antitrust and business law at the University of Arkansas in Fayetteville. Bill's professorial style was laid-back, his courses were loosely structured, and, unlike many law professors, he maintained an easy, informal dialogue with his students.

As she promised, Hillary Rodham took the bar exam in both the District of Columbia and Arkansas. When she flunked the DC exam and passed in Arkansas, she saw it as a sign that she should follow Bill to Fayetteville. But just after Hillary arrived, she and Bill both received calls from legendary civil rights lawyer John Doar, who was heading the House Judiciary Committee's Watergate inquiry. Doar wanted them to help prepare the impeachment case against Richard Nixon. Bill, who had already decided to run for Congress, declined, but Hillary headed to Washington—putting her own stint as an Arkansas law professor on hold. When she finally entered the classroom—nine months later, as a criminal law professor and director of the school's new legal aid clinic—she was more rigorous and a tougher grader than Bill.

IMPEACHING A PRESIDENT: Hillary Rodham was energized by her work with the House Judiciary Committee's presidential impeachment inquiry, relishing the front seat to history that it afforded her. She wrote a crucial memo about what did and did not constitute an impeachable offense. Although the target of the committee's investigation, Richard Nixon, would step down before charges could be brought, the strong case that the team developed against the sitting president helped force his resignation. The experience would also prove useful to Hillary a quarter century later, when her own husband would be impeached.

Photograph by Wally McNamee

RUNNING FOR CONGRESS: In 1974, only a year out of Yale Law School, twenty-eight-year-old Bill Clinton launched a congressional bid in rural northwestern Arkansas. Clinton handily won the Democratic primary but lost the general election to incumbent John Paul Hammerschmidt by a better than expected 52 to 48 percent margin. As a result, Clinton emerged from his first campaign for public office as a viable statewide candidate.

I'm often asked why Bill and I have stayed together.... All I know is that no one understands me better and no one can make me laugh like Bill does.... He is still the most interesting, energizing, and fully alive person I ever met.

—HILLARY RODHAM CLINTON, *Living History,* 2003

WEDDING DAY: Bill repeatedly asked Hillary to marry him, and she always said, "Not yet." Then one day, as Bill drove her to the Fayetteville airport, Hillary mentioned that she liked a small one-bedroom brick house near the university that had a "For Sale" sign in the yard. While Hillary was away for several weeks—visiting friends and pondering her future—Bill bought the house. When Hillary returned to Fayetteville, he said, "Do you remember that house you liked? Well, I bought it, so now you'd better marry me, because I can't live in it by myself."

Hillary finally agreed, and on October 11, 1975, the Reverend Vic Nixon married William Jefferson Clinton and Hillary Diane Rodham in the living room of 930 California Boulevard—now 930 West Clinton Drive. A backyard reception for several hundred guests followed. Hillary decided to keep her maiden name—a source of endless controversy in 1970s Arkansas.

Over the course of the next four decades and at least three very public indiscretions on Bill's part, the complex Clinton-Rodham union would become one of the most publicly analyzed—yet durable—marriages in American public life.

ARKANSAS ATTORNEY GENERAL: Bill Clinton narrowly lost his first political race—for Congress in 1974—but the state Democratic Party recognized him as a rising star. When Bill ran for Arkansas attorney general two years later, the thirty-year-old law professor was the odds-on favorite. He was elected with only minor opposition in the primary and none whatsoever in the general election. While attorney general, Clinton challenged Arkansas's powerful utilities—opposing rate increases and blocking construction of a coal-fired power plant near the Ozark Mountains on environmental grounds. His high-profile defiance of the state's entrenched interests established Bill as a populist figure—and set the stage for his 1978 gubernatorial run.

CAMPAIGN STOP: While running for governor in 1978, the thirty-one-year-old candidate and his wife sing a hymn in an Arkansas church. When David Pryor, the incumbent governor, decided to run for the US Senate, Bill saw his opening. He easily defeated four other candidates for the Democratic nomination. Then he trounced cotton farmer and state Republican chairman Lynn Lowe, garnering nearly two-thirds of the vote. Bill was so sure he would win the general election in heavily Democratic Arkansas that he converted his campaign headquarters into a transition office just after he won the Democratic primary. Clinton later called the general election "uneventful except for the press conference on the steps of the Capitol in which [Lowe's] campaign accused me of being a draft dodger." It was a charge that would be repeated with greater effect during Clinton's 1992 presidential campaign.

SWEARING IN: On January 9, 1979, Hillary Rodham holds the Bible as her husband, age thirty-two, is sworn in as the nation's youngest governor by Arkansas Chief Justice Carleton Harris in the House chamber of the State Capitol. In his inaugural address, Governor Clinton foreshadowed the centrist "Third Way" philosophy that would help him win the presidency. Clinton promised to promote equal opportunity, stem the abuse of government power, cut government waste, protect the environment, help the weak, and expand economic opportunity for the working class. A large "Friends of Bill" contingent from Boys Nation, Georgetown, Yale, and Oxford gathered for the inaugural festivities along with thousands of Arkansans.

GOVERNOR
GRAHAM
Florida

GOVERNOR
RAY
Iowa

BOY GOVERNOR: On February 27, 1979, less than two months into his first term as Arkansas governor, Bill Clinton attends the winter meeting of the National Governors Association—an organization he would later chair. At the conference, Clinton chats with Republican governors Pierre "Pete" du Pont of Delaware and Robert Ray of Iowa. Note Hillary, partially obscured, sitting in the second row.

> *She was a comic figure as a lady lawyer. She tried to look good when she went to court, and she would put on some awful plastic jewelry and high heels she couldn't walk in.*
>
> —HILLARY RODHAM'S LEGAL SECRETARY, AS QUOTED IN *A Woman in Charge: The Life of Hillary Rodham Clinton*

LAW PARTNER: In 1977, when her husband was Arkansas attorney general, Hillary Rodham joined Little Rock's small but powerful Rose Law Firm, which represented some of Arkansas's largest corporations. Two Rose partners befriended her: Vince Foster, who would later become deputy White House counsel, and Web Hubbell, who would become associate attorney general (and in 1994, a convicted felon). Hillary was the 160-year-old firm's first-ever female associate. After Bill was elected governor, she became Rose's first female partner.

Professional women were an anomaly in 1970s Arkansas, and Hillary, who was raised and educated to make her own way in the world, suffered persistent criticism about her career, her use of her maiden name, and her general appearance. In fact, Hillary Rodham never wanted to be a corporate lawyer. She was much more comfortable with public policy law, but she quickly realized that she couldn't rely on her husband for financial stability. Bill, who cared little about money, earned only $26,500 a year as state attorney general and only $35,000 as governor—and he risked unemployment every two years. During her fifteen years at the Rose Law Firm, Hillary earned much more than her husband, and in 1978–79 she made money on the side trading cattle futures under the tutelage of lawyer, trader, and raconteur Jim Blair. In ten months, Blair turned Hillary's $1,000 investment into a $100,000 windfall. Hillary's 10,000 percent return would later raise questions—as would Bill and Hillary's contemporaneous investment in the Whitewater Development Corporation.

ESCORTS: On July 22, 1979, Bill and Hillary accompany First Lady Rosalynn Carter as she tours a cooperative vegetable market in Pine Bluff, Arkansas. Bill Clinton and President Jimmy Carter—a former Southern governor himself—were on friendly terms until 1980, when the Democratic president broke a pledge to Clinton and transported 25,000 Cuban refugees—part of the 125,000-person Mariel boatlift—from South Florida to Fort Chaffee, Arkansas.

Most of the Marielitos were processed and released in a fairly orderly fashion, but on May 29, 1980, approximately 1,000 Cubans broke out of Fort Chaffee and started marching toward the nearby town of Barling. Two days later, rioters burned four buildings inside the military compound. Bill did a good job of containing the incident, but the notion that a Democratic governor and his Democratic president failed to protect the people of Arkansas—deftly exploited by Clinton's Republican opponent, Frank White—contributed to Clinton's 1980 reelection defeat.

HILLARY'S STYLE: A photograph from the Clinton family album, hand-dated February 13, 1979, shows Hillary shopping for a dress, probably in Little Rock. Much has been written about Hillary's apparent inability to dress for success while succeeding anyway. During her early career, the cerebral future first lady, senator, presidential candidate, and secretary of state simply didn't care about her outward appearance. Hillary's attitude would change during her husband's 1992 presidential campaign. "For most of my life, I had paid little attention to my clothes," Hillary would later write. "But during the campaign, some of my friends began a mission to spruce up my appearance.… What they understood, and I didn't, was that a First Lady's appearance matters. I was no longer representing only myself. I was asking the American people to let me represent them."

CHELSEA MORNING: Bill and Hillary's only child, Chelsea Victoria Clinton, arrived on February 27, 1980. The Clintons chose Chelsea's name six months before she was conceived—when they heard folksinger Judy Collins's version of "Chelsea Morning" as they strolled through London's Chelsea district during their 1978 Christmas vacation. Chelsea's conception and birth were both difficult. Hillary suffered from endometriosis, a gynecological condition that complicates conception. And when Chelsea arrived three weeks prematurely, she was in breech, requiring an emergency cesarian section. At the time, Little Rock hospitals did not allow fathers in the delivery room when surgery was required. Predictably, the governor talked his way in and held Hillary's hand throughout the procedure. **Above**, Bill and Hillary on the day they brought Chelsea home to the Arkansas governor's mansion.

MISSTEP: Governor Clinton speaks to a joint session of the Arkansas legislature in 1980. In the gubernatorial election later that year his opponent, Democrat–turned–Republican Frank White, leveraged two contentious issues to unseat the young governor: the 1980 Cuban refugee riots at Fort Chaffee and Clinton's unpopular decision to raise car registration fees to improve Arkansas's highway system. Those issues, combined with Ronald Reagan's forty-four-state presidential sweep—including Arkansas—led to Clinton's defeat. Bill Clinton became only the second Democratic gubernatorial candidate to lose an Arkansas election since 1872. "It was like a death in the family," remembers Max Brantley, editor of the *Arkansas Times*. "He was really destroyed after losing that election."

HILLARY 1980: While Hillary Rodham was a partner at the Rose Law Firm, President Carter appointed her to the board of the Legal Services Corporation—a nonprofit agency established during the Nixon administration to provide free legal assistance to people who could not afford a lawyer. As board chair, Hillary tripled federal funding for the program, then successfully defended her budget against proposed cuts by the incoming Reagan administration. During her husband's first administration, Hillary also chaired Arkansas's Rural Health Advisory Committee, where she secured federal funds to expand medical facilities in Arkansas's poorest areas—the future first lady's first foray into government health care.

You know, this is extremely complicated, this family.

—Virginia Clinton Kelley during a 1992 campaign interview

CHELSEA, GRANDMA, AND UNCLE ROGER: A 1981 photo of the thirty-four-year-old former governor—at the time, an attorney with the Little Rock firm of Wright, Lindsey and Jennings—with one-and-a-half-year-old Chelsea; Bill's thrice-widowed mother, Virginia Cassidy Blythe Clinton Dwire (soon to be Kelley); and Bill's half-brother from his mother's second marriage, Roger Clinton Jr., who was twenty-five when this photo was snapped.

The future president came from what has to be described as a difficult family: his biological father was a womanizing bigamist; the stepfather who raised him was a violent alcoholic; and his half-brother, Roger, would become yet another entrant in a long line of troubled presidential brothers.

In 1984, while Bill Clinton was serving his second term as governor, the Arkansas state police videotaped Roger selling cocaine to a police informer. Bill could have intervened, but he recused himself on ethical grounds—a decision that deeply wounded his mother. Roger served eighteen months in jail for cocaine possession. In 2001, during his final days as president, Bill would pardon his half-brother for the cocaine conviction. But by that time, Roger, who pursued a singing and acting career, was under investigation for attempting to influence the presidential pardon process on behalf of several other convicted criminals, including a reputed Mafia soldier serving a forty-five-year sentence for heroin trafficking.

REDEMPTION TRAIL: Bill and Hillary campaign with Chelsea on May 31, 1982. When he was voted out of office in 1980, Clinton nominally spent his two years in the wilderness working at the Little Rock law firm of Wright, Lindsey and Jennings. But in reality, he devoted much of his time to rebuilding his political base. He was brilliantly assisted in this effort by Betsey Wright, a friend of Hillary's from the McGovern campaign and Clinton's future gubernatorial chief of staff. In 1982, the Clintons returned to the campaign trail determined to regain the governor's mansion. "Since I dug my own grave," Clinton later wrote, "the only sensible thing to do seemed to be to start climbing out."

PRIMARY VICTORY: The former Arkansas governor and his wife celebrate Clinton's victory in the Democratic runoff on June 8, 1982. Clinton finished first among five candidates with 42 percent of the primary vote. Then he defeated former lieutenant governor Joe Purcell in the runoff election, earning him the right to face incumbent governor Frank White—the man who had defeated him two years earlier. Fortunately for Clinton, White committed a series of embarrassing gaffes during his two-year term. His heavy-handed effort to shut down Hillary's rural health clinics was rebuked by the public. His support for a bill requiring Arkansas public schools to teach creationism was ridiculed. And at a press conference announcing an Arkansas trade mission to Japan and Taiwan, he exhibited a shaky grasp of world geography when he told reporters that he would be delighted to visit the Middle East.

THE CHALLENGER: The Democratic nominee tells reporters at a news conference in Little Rock on Wednesday, June 9, 1982, that he wants to debate incumbent governor Frank White. White declined, but to no avail. Clinton won the general election decisively with 55 percent of the vote, regaining the post he lost two years earlier.

Photograph by Greg Smith

VICTORY DANCE: Bill and Hillary celebrate on January 11, 1983, the day Bill Clinton—Arkansas's defeated fortieth governor—returned to power as its forty-second chief executive. Clinton learned some hard political lessons during his first term. The most important: If voters truly despise an idea—such as the governor's first-term initiative to raise car registration fees to fix Arkansas's crumbling highway system—it doesn't matter if you're right or not. It won't work.

With help from his wife and his chief of staff, Betsey Wright, Bill applied that lesson well—picking his issues and spending his political capital carefully. Clinton would be elected to a third two-year term in 1984, then two more four-year terms, making him one of Arkansas's two longest-serving governors.

MOMMY AND ME: A May 13, 1984, portrait of Hillary and Chelsea, four years old at the time. Chelsea grew up in the Arkansas governor's mansion, living there until she was twelve. Then she lived in the White House until she left for Stanford University. Although Bill and Hillary worked long hours and Chelsea was surrounded by nannies, aides, and security personnel, Bill and Hillary's only child would develop and maintain a close, loving relationship with both parents—even during Bill's embarrassing sex scandals. A quarter century after this photo was snapped, Hillary would choose Chelsea to introduce her at the 2008 Democratic Convention. The poised twenty-eight-year-old, who campaigned for Hillary on more than one hundred college campuses, would narrate a loving video tribute before introducing "my mother and my hero."

DADDY'S GIRL: Bill and Chelsea—six years old at the time—after the governor cast his vote during the Democratic primary on May 27, 1986. In his fifth run for the Arkansas governor's office, the popular incumbent was challenged by two fellow Democrats: former segregationist governor Orval Faubus and the African American chief of Arkansas's anti-poverty agency, W. Dean Goldsby. Clinton prevailed with more than 60 percent of the primary vote. Then, in the general election, he thrashed his old nemesis, Republican Frank White, for the third and final time. In 1986, Arkansas lengthened its governor's term of office from two to four years, so Clinton would run for the post only one more time—in 1990.

Photograph by Danny Johnston

FOURTH TERM: On January 13, 1987, the Clintons, **above**, arrive at Bill's fourth inaugural ball in Little Rock. Then Bill and Hillary, **right**, share a dance.

 After more than a decade in Arkansas, Hillary's life, as she approached middle age, had turned out differently than she once expected. In the early 1970s, she was considered the irreverent voice of her generation, the brilliant star of a law school that graduated presidents, senators, and Supreme Court justices, a fresh face in American public policy and a feminist paragon. But Hillary had evolved into a corporate lawyer in a midsized Southern town who (publicly at least) played an adjunct role to her husband—and was not even allowed to keep her maiden name because in Arkansas, that proved too controversial. While she made important contributions to Arkansas's health care and education systems, chaired the Legal Services Corporation, and supported her family financially, Hillary Rodham Clinton was still, by her own standards, a big fish in a small backwater pond. In five years, all that would change.

TELEVISED GAFFE: As an up-and-comer with national potential, the four-term governor of Arkansas was tapped to nominate Massachusetts Governor Michael Dukakis at the 1988 Democratic National Convention in Atlanta. It was a rare nationwide forum for the young governor, but Clinton squandered the opportunity, delivering an overly long thirty-two-minute speech that first bored and then irritated convention delegates. Clinton's only applause line was "in conclusion." It should have been a humiliating public defeat for Clinton, but in trademark fashion he bounced back quickly, engaging the press and laughing off his nationally televised disaster. "That should have told you something about Bill Clinton," remembers NBC newsman Tom Brokaw. "He would make the big mistake, but then he would crawl out of it in his own endearing fashion."

MAKING LIGHT OF THE SITUATION: A week after his disastrous nominating speech at the Democratic National Convention, Clinton appeared on the popular late-night television program, *The Tonight Show Starring Johnny Carson*. A master comedian, Carson parodied Clinton's speech with a hilarious four-minute introduction that included Bill's entire biography and a short history of Arkansas. Then Clinton effectively made fun of himself and played his saxophone with Doc Severinsen and the NBC Orchestra. It was, in the words of Hillary Clinton, "yet another comeback."

Photograph by Bob Galbraith

HAPPIER TIMES: Vince and Lisa Foster join the governor and Hillary at a Little Rock theater premiere in 1988. Vincent Foster Jr. was Bill's boyhood friend and Hillary's mentor at the Rose Law Firm. When Bill and Hillary moved to Washington in 1992, they tapped the highly respected attorney as deputy White House counsel. But Foster was constitutionally unsuited for the vicious nature of Washington politics. When Zoe Baird, Clinton's attorney general nominee, was dropped for employing illegal aliens, Foster blamed himself for not vetting her sufficiently. When the Clintons were savaged in the press for firing White House Travel Office employees, he shouldered the responsibility.

Increasingly anxious and depressed, Foster could not, in his own mind, return to Arkansas as a failure. He knew he needed help, but felt he could not consult a psychiatrist or take anti-depression medication without attracting negative public attention.

The breaking point may have come when *The Wall Street Journal*, a newspaper Foster respected, ran a series of highly critical editorials, including one entitled, "Who is Vince Foster?," and another, "Vincent Foster's Victory," that compared the courtly Arkansas lawyer to disgraced Iran-Contra operative Oliver North. A month after the second article appeared Foster paid the family bills, ate lunch in his office, then drove to a suburban Virginia park, where he fatally shot himself. In a torn-up suicide note/resignation letter later found in his briefcase, forty-eight-year-old Foster wrote, in part, "The WSJ editors lie without consequence. I was not meant for the job or the spotlight of public life in Washington. Here, ruining people is considered sport."

THIRD WAY: Bill Clinton delivers the keynote address at the Democratic Leadership Council convention in Cleveland, Ohio, on May 6, 1991. Founded in 1985 in response to Ronald Reagan's massive defeat of Democratic presidential candidate Walter Mondale, the DLC argued that the Democratic Party should shift away from the liberal stance it adopted in the 1960s in favor of a more centrist coalition. Clinton's election as president the following year would validate the DLC's "Third Way" philosophy.

Photograph by Mark Duncan

The country is headed in the wrong direction fast, slipping behind, losing our way. And all we have out of Washington is status quo paralysis. No vision, no action. Just neglect, selfishness, and division.

— BILL CLINTON'S ANNOUNCEMENT SPEECH IN LITTLE ROCK, ARKANSAS, 1991

WHITE HOUSE RUN: On October 3, 1991, outside the Old State House in Little Rock, Bill Clinton announces his presidential bid. Four years earlier, when New York governor Mario Cuomo dropped out of the 1988 race and frontrunner Gary Hart was derailed by a sex scandal, Clinton seriously considered a run. He went so far as to schedule a press conference to announce his intention, but at the last minute, he decided that Chelsea was still too young to endure a presidential campaign. (He may also have been discouraged by the list of reputed paramours that chief of staff Betsey Wright showed him.) By 1991, however, Chelsea was eleven, and Clinton decided it was his time. Hillary, who had spent more than a decade and a half in Arkansas, relished the idea of returning to the national stage and she stood solidly behind Bill's decision.

Photograph by Cynthia Johnson

It's Christmas. We all know in The Christmas Carol, *George Bush is Scrooge, but the Democrats can't afford to be "The Ghost of Christmas Past."*

— BILL CLINTON'S CLOSING REMARKS DURING THE FIRST DEMOCRATIC CANDIDATES DEBATE, 1991

THE CANDIDATE: On December 15, 1991, Clinton shows up early for the first nationally televised Democratic presidential candidates debate in Washington, DC. During the ninety-minute parley Clinton would face, **l–r** as represented by their photographs, former Massachusetts senator Paul Tsongas, Iowa senator Tom Harkin, Nebraska senator Bob Kerry, former (and future) California governor Jerry Brown, and Virginia governor Douglas Wilder. The acknowledged front-runner at the time, New York governor Mario Cuomo, did not attend, and after a long period of vacillation that earned him the sobriquet "Hamlet on the Hudson," he would eventually decide not to run. Although Jerry Brown dominated the debate with repeated attacks on political corruption, Clinton, the more moderate candidate, scored points when he outlined his well-considered strategies to revive America's struggling middle class.

Photograph by Robert McNeely

FLOWERS POWER: Three weeks before the critical 1992 New Hampshire primary, the Clinton campaign was rocked by scandal. On January 27, 1992, Arkansas state employee and cabaret singer Gennifer Flowers, **above**, called a New York City press conference to field questions about her alleged twelve-year affair with the presidential hopeful. Bill and Hillary responded with an appearance on a post-Superbowl edition of *60 Minutes*, watched by fifty million Americans. Although Bill did not categorically deny an affair with Flowers, Hillary staunchly supported her husband. "You know, I'm not sitting here—some little woman standing by my man like Tammy Wynette," said Hillary. "I'm sitting here because I love him, and I respect him, and I honor what he's been through and what we've been through together."

Although Hillary was criticized for disrespecting Tammy Wynette, and Bill did not win in New Hampshire, he came close enough—only seven points behind former Massachusetts senator Paul Tsongas—to keep his campaign alive. Six years later, in a deposition he gave during the Paula Jones sexual harassment case, Clinton would finally acknowledge that he did have sexual relations with Flowers—once, he said, in 1977. At **right**, Clinton high fives supporters during an election night party in Merrimack, New Hampshire.

Photographs by Ricard Drew (top) and Ron Frehm (right)

CONTROVERSIAL REMARK: On March 16, 1992, Hillary campaigns at the Busy Bee Restaurant, a Polish-American diner on Chicago's Northwest Side. During the previous evening's raucous Democratic candidates debate, former California governor Jerry Brown accused Governor Clinton of funneling profitable Arkansas state business to Hillary's law firm. When a reporter at the Busy Bee raised Brown's accusations, Hillary responded with a controversial riposte that foreshadowed her role as an activist first lady and insulted stay-at-home moms across America. "I suppose I could have stayed at home and baked cookies and had teas," replied Hillary, "but what I decided was to fulfill my profession which I entered before my husband was in public life." The remark—lauded by some, criticized by others—would dog her for the rest of the campaign.

Photograph by Steve Liss

HELP FROM MOM: On the second day of the Democratic National Convention in New York, seventy-three-year-old Dorothy Rodham helps daughter Hillary prepare for the evening's festivities. Deemed a long shot at the beginning of the primary season, Bill Clinton proved an adept campaigner and wrapped up the Democratic nomination in early June. At the convention, 3,372 of the party's 4,276 delegates would cast their ballots for the Arkansas governor who surprised pundits when he chose another young southerner, Senator Al Gore of Tennessee, as his running mate.

Photograph by Ron Frehm

THE NOMINEE: On the final night of the four-day 1992 Democratic National Convention at New York's Madison Square Garden, the standard bearer and his wife, **left**, acknowledge applause from the delegates. Democratic National Committee chair (later Commerce Secretary) Ron Brown ran a tight, reasonably unified, and effectively messaged convention with standout speeches by Jesse Jackson, New York governor Mario Cuomo, and Georgia governor Zell Miller. Miller took a sharp poke at Republican vice-presidential candidate Dan Quayle, saying, "We can't all be born rich, handsome, and lucky. And that's why we have a Democratic Party." Also effective: a short biographical film entitled *The Man From Hope* produced by Clinton's Hollywood friends Harry Thomason and Linda Bloodworth-Thomason, producers of a popular television series, *Designing Women*.

The highlight for Bill Clinton, however, came on the convention's third night, when Democratic delegates voted. First-in-the-alphabet Alabama deferred to Arkansas, allowing Bill's home state to cast the initial votes. The Arkansans chose Bill's mother, Virginia, to speak for the delegation. Virginia, who often told her son that he would grow up to be president, said very simply, "Arkansas proudly casts our forty-eight votes for our favorite son and my son, Bill Clinton."

"I wonder what Mother was thinking and feeling…," Clinton later wrote. "Whether her mind wandered back forty-six years to the twenty-three-year-old widow who gave me life, or back over all the troubles she has borne with a bright smile to give me and my brother as normal a life as possible."

Shortly before Bill spoke, third party candidate Ross Perot, who briefly led the race, withdrew from the campaign. (He would re-enter eleven weeks later.) Perot's withdrawal, combined with an unusually large "convention bounce," put Clinton on top of the polls as Bill and Hillary left Manhattan for campaign stops in New Jersey and Pennsylvania, **above**.

Photographs by Les Stone

CAMPAIGN TRAIL: Facing page, top, and **above**: Following the triumphant 1992 Democratic National Convention, candidates Bill Clinton and Al Gore, wives in tow, embarked on a six-day bus tour across New Jersey, Pennsylvania, West Virginia, Kentucky, Indiana, Ohio, Illinois and Missouri—states with a combined 117 electoral votes. Their goal: to reposition Democrats as the party of small-town, middle-class values.

The Bush campaign and its surrogates countered with a series of character attacks. During the course of the campaign, they would accuse Clinton of rampant infidelity, draft dodging, organizing Vietnam War protests in England, meeting communists during a 1969 student trip to Russia, and smoking marijuana. (Absurdly, Clinton would admit only to puffing, not inhaling, marijuana, and then only beyond America's borders.)

The Bush campaign, which crippled its 1988 opponent Michael Dukakis with the "Willie Horton attack ads" that depicted the Democratic governor as soft on crime—expected these strikes to be decisive. But without Lee Atwater, Bush's hyper-aggressive campaign strategist

who died in 1991, the attacks fell short. Bush—who had an 80-plus percent approval rating when the Gulf War ended the previous year—made another tactical error when he emphasized his foreign policy successes during an economic downturn. In the end, Americans were more interested in pocketbook issues than Clinton's moral failings or Bush's overseas achievements. Even after Perot reentered the race in October, the Clinton campaign stayed on top by pointing out Bush's "read my lips" flip-flop on new taxes, and more importantly, by heeding Clinton campaign manager James Carville's maxim: "It's the economy, stupid." **Facing page, bottom**: Clinton campaigning in Chicago in October 1992.

Photographs by Andrew Lichtenstein (facing page, top), Robert McNeely (facing page, bottom) and Ron Haviv (above)

VICTORY PARTY: On November 3, 1992, Bill Clinton and his running mate, Al Gore, **above**, received 45 million votes—only 43 percent of the ballots cast in the three-way race, but enough for the Democratic ticket to take thirty-two states and the District of Columbia. The election ended an era when Republicans had won five of the six previous presidential elections. Democrats also retained control of both houses of Congress—an executive-legislative dominance that would last only two years.

Clinton learned that he had won the presidency fairly early in the evening. All three networks projected victory for the first baby-boomer chief executive by 9:30 p.m. Incumbent president Bush made his concession call shortly thereafter. Then Bill and Hillary walked from their Little Rock hotel to the Old State House, where Clinton had announced his bid thirteen months earlier. Al and Tipper Gore and a throng of thousands waited for him. "I was overwhelmed when I looked out into the faces of all those people," Clinton later wrote. "I loved seeing my mother's tears of joy, and I hoped that my father was looking down on me with pride." After his acceptance speech, in which he called for "a re-United States," Clinton, **right**, did what he loved best, connecting with the crowd.

Photograph by J. Scott Applewhite (right)

TRIUMPHAL EMBRACE: After delivering his acceptance speech and working the crowd, Bill and Hillary, **left**, took time for a well-earned hug. Perhaps more than any other presidential campaign in modern history, Clinton's 1992 victory was a husband-and-wife effort. At times, Hillary was a lightning rod for controversy, but no one doubted her smarts—or that her support during the Gennifer Flowers imbroglio had saved the campaign. Across the country, Bill told voters that if they elected him, they would get "two for the price of one." But on election night, the question remained: Was America ready for a full-partner first lady?

Photograph by Ralf-Finn Hestoft

LEAVING MOTHER: The president-elect with his mother, Virginia Kelley, **above**, in Little Rock on January 16, 1992, minutes before Clinton delivered his farewell speech to the people of Arkansas. After the speech, Bill and Hillary flew to Charlottesville, Virginia, where they joined Al and Tipper Gore at Thomas Jefferson's historic home, Monticello. Then all four traveled 120 miles together by bus to Washington, retracing Jefferson's 1801 inaugural journey. Virginia joined her son in Washington, and after the inauguration ceremony, Bill took her to the White House Rose Garden to show her the exact spot where, three decades earlier, he had shaken hands with John F. Kennedy.

Photograph by J. David Ake

OATH OF OFFICE: Flanked by his wife and daughter, William Jefferson Clinton takes the oath of office as forty-second president of the United States. Chief Justice William Rehnquist administers the oath on the west steps of the Capitol on Wednesday, January 20, 1993.

Hillary Clinton's suspicious glance at the chief justice anticipates the friction between Rehnquist and the Clintons during the next eight years. Appointed by Richard Nixon in 1971 and elevated to chief justice by Ronald Reagan in 1986, Rehnquist was a staunch conservative. As a Supreme Court clerk, he wrote a memorandum opposing school desegregation during the 1953 *Brown v. Board of Education* deliberations; as a justice, he opposed the legalization of abortion in *Roe v. Wade*. In 1995, under the special prosecutor law, Rehnquist would appoint three very conservative federal judges to select an independent counsel to investigate the Clintons. Their choice would be conservative zealot Ken Starr.

Photograph by Ed Reinke

FIRST INAUGURAL ADDRESS

Bill Clinton, Washington, January 20, 1993

My fellow citizens, today we celebrate the mystery of American renewal. This ceremony is held in the depth of winter, but by the words we speak and the faces we show the world, we force the spring[1], a spring reborn in the world's oldest democracy that brings forth the vision and courage to reinvent America. When our founders boldly declared America's independence to the world and our purposes to the Almighty, they knew that America, to endure, would have to change; not change for change's sake, but change to preserve America's ideals: life, liberty, the pursuit of happiness. Though we marched to the music of our time, our mission is timeless. Each generation of Americans must define what it means to be an American.

On behalf of our nation, I salute my predecessor, President Bush, for his half-century of service to America. And I thank the millions of men and women whose steadfastness and sacrifice triumphed over depression, fascism, and communism.

Today, a generation raised in the shadows of the cold war assumes new responsibilities in a world warmed by the sunshine of freedom, but threatened still by ancient hatreds and new plagues. Raised in unrivaled prosperity, we inherit an economy that is still the world's strongest but is weakened by business failures, stagnant wages, increasing inequality, and deep divisions among our own people.

---

[1] Three weeks before Clinton's inauguration, Father Tim Healy, the former president of Clinton's alma mater, Georgetown University (later president of the New York Public Library), wrote a letter to the president-elect in which he hoped that Clinton's election would "force the spring." Bill and Hillary liked the phrase and incorporated it into the inaugural address. Sadly, Healy died before he could hear it.

When George Washington first took the oath I have just sworn to uphold, news traveled slowly across the land by horseback and across the ocean by boat. Now, the sights and sounds of this ceremony are broadcast instantaneously to billions around the world. Communications and commerce are global. Investment is mobile. Technology is almost magical. And ambition for a better life is now universal.

We earn our livelihood in America today in peaceful competition with people all across the Earth. Profound and powerful forces are shaking and remaking our world. And the urgent question of our time is whether we can make change our friend and not our enemy. This new world has already enriched the lives of millions of Americans who are able to compete and win in it. But when most people are working harder for less; when others cannot work at all; when the cost of health care devastates families

There is nothing wrong with America that cannot be cured by what is right with America.

and threatens to bankrupt our enterprises, great and small; when the fear of crime robs law-abiding citizens of their freedom; and when millions of poor children cannot even imagine the lives we are calling them to lead, we have not made change our friend.

We know we have to face hard truths and take strong steps, but we have not done so; instead, we have drifted. And that drifting has eroded our resources, fractured our economy, and shaken our confidence. Though our challenges are fearsome, so are our strengths. Americans have ever been a restless, questing, hopeful people. And we must bring to our task today the vision and will of those who came before us. From our Revolution to the Civil War, to the Great Depression, to the civil rights movement, our people have always mustered the determination to construct from these crises the pillars of our history. Thomas Jefferson believed that to preserve the very foundations of our nation, we would need dramatic change from time to time. Well, my fellow Americans, this is our time. Let us embrace it.

Our democracy must be not only the envy of the world, but the engine of our own renewal. There is nothing wrong with America that cannot be cured by what is right with America. And so today we pledge an end to the era of deadlock and drift, and a new season of American renewal has begun.

To renew America, we must be bold. We must do what no generation has had to do before. We must invest more in our own people, in their jobs, and in their future, and at the same time cut our massive debt.[2] And we must do so in a world in which we must compete for every opportunity. It will not be easy. It will require sacrifice, but it can be done and done fairly, not choosing sacrifice for its own sake but for our own sake. We must provide for our nation the way a family provides for its children.

Our founders saw themselves in the light of posterity. We can do no less. Anyone who has ever watched a child's eyes wander into sleep knows what posterity is. Posterity is the world to come, the world for whom we hold our ideals, from whom we have borrowed our planet, and to whom we bear sacred responsibility. We must do what America does best: offer more opportunity to all and demand more responsibility from all. It is time to break the bad habit of expecting something for nothing from our government or from each other. Let us all take more responsibility, not only for ourselves and our families, but for our communities and our country.

Let us resolve to reform our politics so that power and privilege no longer shout down the voice of the people.

To renew America, we must revitalize our democracy. This beautiful capital, like every capital since the dawn of civilization, is often a place of intrigue and calculation. Powerful people maneuver for position and worry endlessly about who is in and who is out, who is up and who is down, forgetting those people whose toil and sweat sends us here and pays our way. Americans deserve better. And in this city today there are people who want to do better. And so I say to all of you here: Let us resolve to reform our politics so that power and privilege no longer shout down the voice of the people. Let us put aside personal advantage so that we can feel the pain and see the promise of America. Let us resolve to make our government a place for what Franklin Roosevelt called bold, persistent experimentation, a government for our tomorrows, not our yesterdays. Let us give this capital back to the people to whom it belongs.

To renew America, we must meet challenges abroad as well as at home. There is no longer a clear division between what is foreign and what is domestic. The world economy, the world environment, the world AIDS crisis, the world arms race, they affect us all. Today, as an older order passes, the new world is more free but less stable. Communism's

---

[2] The national debt increased nearly three hundred percent during the Ronald Reagan and George H. W. Bush administrations (FY 1981–1993). It would rise less than 50 percent during the Clinton presidency (FY 1994–2001), and in his last four budgets, Clinton would show a surplus.

collapse has called forth old animosities and new dangers. Clearly, America must continue to lead the world we did so much to make.

While America rebuilds at home, we will not shrink from the challenges nor fail to seize the opportunities of this new world. Together with our friends and allies, we will work to shape change, lest it engulf us. When our vital interests are challenged or the will and conscience of the international community is defied, we will act, with peaceful diplomacy whenever possible, with force when necessary. The brave Americans serving our Nation today in the Persian Gulf[3], in Somalia[4], and wherever else they stand are testament to our resolve. But our greatest strength is the power of our ideas, which are still new in many lands. Across the world we see them embraced, and we rejoice. Our hopes, our hearts, our hands are with those on every continent who are building democracy and freedom. Their cause is America's cause.

As we stand at the edge of the twenty-first century, let us begin anew with energy and hope, with faith and discipline.

The American people have summoned the change we celebrate today. You have raised your voices in an unmistakable chorus. You have cast your votes in historic numbers.[5] And you have changed the face of Congress, the presidency, and the political process itself. Yes, you, my fellow Americans, have forced the spring. Now we must do the work the season demands. To that work I now turn with all the authority of my office. I ask the Congress to join with me. But no president, no congress, no government can undertake this mission alone.

My fellow Americans, you, too, must play your part in our renewal. I challenge a new generation of young Americans to a season of service: to act on your idealism by helping troubled children, keeping company with those in need, reconnecting our torn communities. There is so much to be done—enough, indeed, for millions of others who are still

[3] After the 1991 Gulf War, US forces remained in the Persian Gulf region to maintain order and contain Iraqi dictator Saddam Hussein.

[4] In December 1992, President George H. W. Bush deployed more than 10,000 US troops to Somalia in response to a humanitarian crisis precipitated by a civil war. The US contingent, part of a larger United Nations force, grew during the first year of the Clinton administration, but was, for the most part, withdrawn five months after the October 1993 Battle of Mogadishu, better known as the Black Hawk Down incident.

[5] The number of votes cast in the 1992 presidential election was the largest to date.

young in spirit to give of themselves in service, too. In serving, we recognize a simple but powerful truth: we need each other, and we must care for one another.

Today we do more than celebrate America. We rededicate ourselves to the very idea of America—an idea born in revolution and renewed through two centuries of challenge; an idea tempered by the knowledge that, but for fate, we, the fortunate, and the unfortunate might have been each other; an idea ennobled by the faith that our nation can summon from its myriad diversity the deepest measure of unity; an idea infused with the conviction that America's long, heroic journey must go forever upward.

And so, my fellow Americans, as we stand at the edge of the twenty-first century, let us begin anew with energy and hope, with faith and discipline. And let us work until our work is done. The Scripture says, "And let us not be weary in well doing: for in due season we shall reap, if we faint not." From this joyful mountaintop of celebration we hear a call to service in the valley. We have heard the trumpets. We have changed the guard. And now, each in our own way, and with God's help, we must answer the call.

Thank you, and God bless you all.

FIRST COUPLE: The new president and first lady, **above**, walk down Pennsylvania Avenue during the inaugural parade. Bill and Hillary rode most of the way from the Capitol to the White House, but with reluctant permission from the Secret Service, they hopped out of their limousine at the Treasury Building and walked to the reviewing stand in front of the White House. There, they watched a three-hour inaugural parade that included six bands from Arkansas alone. Later, the First Couple, **right**, danced at all eleven inaugural balls and did not return to the White House until two in the morning. "It was fascinating," Hillary later wrote, "to watch my husband that week as he literally became President before my eyes."

Photographs by Steve Liss (above) and Larry Downing (facing page)

ABORTION RIGHTS: On January 22, 1993—the third day of his administration and the twentieth anniversary of the Supreme Court's landmark *Roe v. Wade* decision legalizing abortion in the United States—Clinton, with Vice President Al Gore (and Roughrider Teddy Roosevelt) looking on, signs an executive order lifting five major abortion restrictions imposed during the Reagan and Bush administrations.

With a stroke of his pen, the new president lifted the ban on abortion counseling in federally-financed clinics, removed restrictions on federal financing for research using fetal tissue, eased abortion policy in military hospitals, and reversed Reagan's prohibition on aid to international family-planning programs that offered access to abortions. Hours earlier, more than 75,000 angry anti-abortion demonstrators marked the *Roe v. Wade* anniversary with a rally across the street from the White House.

DON'T ASK, DON'T TELL: A week after he eased abortion restrictions, Clinton—who was bashed as a draft dodger during the 1992 campaign—announced a plan to lift the ban on gays serving in the US military. Tackling both abortion rights and gays in the military during the first few days of his presidency helped coalesce forceful conservative opposition to Clinton from the get-go. "Awful mistake on the president's part," recalled General Tony McPeak, who was Air Force chief of staff at the time. "To single out the gays-in-the-military thing as the number one problem on his national security agenda was a misjudgment …and I'm sure he would agree. He got taken to the cleaners, and it wasn't a nice scene to watch." Clinton's third out-of-the-gate initiative, the Family and Medical Leave Act, which gave workers time off from their job when a baby was born or a family member fell ill, was far more popular. "More people would mention it," Clinton later wrote, "than any other bill I signed."

Photograph by Ron Edmonds

ADVICE FROM JACKIE: On January 26, 1993, six days after Bill's inauguration, Hillary and a few staffers took a commercial shuttle flight from Washington, DC, to New York City—the first and last time Hillary tried to fly commercial during her White House years. The official purpose of her trip was to receive an award for her work on children's issues and to visit New York's PS 115, **above**, to promote a voluntary tutoring program. But Hillary also sought advice from her predecessor and personal idol, Jacqueline Kennedy Onassis.

Over lunch at Jackie's Fifth Avenue apartment, the former first lady subtly warned Hillary that charismatic politicians such as Hillary's husband could become assassination targets. She also stressed the importance of raising Chelsea as normally as possible under the circumstances. "You've got to protect Chelsea at all costs," advised the former first lady, who raised two young children in the White House. "Surround her with friends and family, but don't spoil her. Don't let her think she's someone special or entitled." Hillary and Jackie would maintain a close friendship until Jackie died from cancer the following year. The photograph, **left**, was taken six months after Hillary's initial meeting with Jackie—during the Clinton's 1993 summer vacation on Martha's Vineyard, Massachusetts.

> *By their fifth day in the White House, the Clintons were swamped in controversy over homosexuality, abortion, and Hillary's hidden hand.*
>
> — CARL BERNSTEIN in *A WOMAN IN CHARGE: THE LIFE OF HILLARY RODHAM CLINTON*

ORGANIZED CHAOS: On February 15, 1993, the president, Al Gore, White House Chief of Staff Thomas "Mack" McLarty, de facto press secretary George Stephanopoulos, and a raft of White House staffers gather to discuss Clinton's first address to a joint session of Congress—a so-called "Administration Goals Speech" that the president would deliver two days later. The White House was still reeling from the forced withdrawal of Clinton's attorney general designee, Zoe Baird, and the team needed a home run. Clinton tended to rewrite, edit, and rehearse important speeches until the last possible moment, driving everyone around him crazy in the process. In Hillary's words, "He's never met a sentence he couldn't fool with"—and this time was no exception.

Photograph by Robert McNeely

Our nation needs a new direction.... We need to break the old habits of both political parties in Washington. We must say that there can be no more something for nothing, and we are all in this together.

— BILL CLINTON'S FIRST ADDRESS TO A
JOINT SESSION OF CONGRESS, 1993

PLAN OF ACTION: On February 17, 1993, Vice President Al Gore watches Bill Clinton deliver his first address to a joint session of Congress. In his speech, the president set forth a very ambitious agenda: revive the economy, reduce unemployment, eliminate the deficit, pass the North American Free Trade Agreement, raise taxes for the wealthiest Americans, create a national service program for young people, "end welfare as we know it," reduce crime by putting 100,000 additional police officers on the street, and pass a national health care plan. Despite a rocky start and relentless personal attacks from his opponents over the next eight years, Clinton would—with the notable exception of health care reform—accomplish every one of these formidable goals during his two terms in office.

I think we're going to get killed. We'll need at least four to five years to put together a package that will pass Congress.

— Ira Magaziner, co-chair of Clinton's Task Force to Reform Health Care, 1993

PARTNERS IN HEALTHCARE: The Clintons embrace in the Capitol after the president successfully delivered his first address to a joint session of Congress. Clinton's impressive list of administration goals prominently featured an overhaul of the nation's health care system. Three weeks earlier, Bill announced that Hillary would chair a health care task force that would produce reform legislation in one hundred days. Virtually no one except Bill thought such a complex task could be achieved in the time allotted—certainly not Hillary or her second-in-command, Ira Magaziner. New York Governor Mario Cuomo, one of America's canniest politicians at the time, put it more bluntly, "What did you do to make your husband so mad at you?" he asked Hillary, "He'd have to be awfully upset about something to put you in charge of such a thankless task."

Photograph by Robert McNeely

JOCKS: The president—who often battled his weight—and his Secret Service escort jog through central Washington on March 3, 1993. Clinton's sweatshirt touts a nonprofit organization that encourages students to stay in school and helped inspire Clinton's signature AmeriCorps volunteer program. "I met a lot of interesting people on those runs," Clinton later wrote, "When the Secret Service finally asked me to stop because of security concerns, I did, but I missed it."

AND SOCKS: Later the same month, Clinton takes First Cat, Socks, out for some exercise. When Socks—a stray Chelsea adopted in Arkansas—lived at the governor's mansion, he was an outdoor cat. But when the Clintons moved to Washington, they soon learned that Socks could easily slip through the White House fence into DC traffic. From that point forward, the First Cat only went out on a leash. Socks' life would become increasingly stressful during the second Clinton administration when the president adopted a chocolate Labrador retriever named Buddy. "Socks despised Buddy," Hillary later wrote, "We tried so hard to convince them to get along. But if we left them in the same room, we inevitably came back to find Socks with his back arched, hissing at Buddy, who was intent on chasing the cat under the couch."

RUSSIAN TUTOR: On March 8, 1993, former president Richard Nixon returned to the White House to give Clinton the benefit of his long experience with Russia. At the time, Clinton was preparing for his first summit meeting with Russian President Boris Yeltsin. Nixon had just returned from a two-week trip to the former Soviet Union that included a long sit-down with Yeltsin. Clinton listened carefully to Nixon's insights into Yeltsin's character and his analysis of the Russian premier's precarious political situation. Both presidents agreed that it was important to support Yeltsin during the early post-Soviet period. "President Nixon gave me a lot of good ideas," said Clinton, who would become close friends with Yeltsin.

Photograph by Robert McNeely

THE POLITICS OF MEANING: The first lady with Texas governor Ann Richards at the Liz Carpenter Lecture in Austin, Texas, on April 6, 1993. At the time, Hillary's father, Hugh Rodham, was lingering close to death after a severe stroke, and the first lady desperately wanted to skip the event. But Liz Carpenter, Lady Bird Johnson's former press secretary, convinced her to come. Hillary, who was understandably emotional, ended up ruminating publicly on the deathbed repentance of George H. W. Bush's political hatchet man, Lee Atwater, who had died from brain cancer two years earlier. "We need a new politics of meaning," said the first lady, "We need a new ethos of individual responsibility and caring." Hillary's father passed away the day after the lecture. A few days after that, the *New York Times Magazine* mocked the first lady's remarks as "New Age jargon."

OUTSIDE HELP: Clinton listens to his new presidential counselor, David Gergen, during a Rose Garden press conference on May 30, 1993. After a rocky four-month start when the White House was perceived as massively disorganized and Clinton was viewed as a moderate lurching leftward, the president reached out to Gergen—a former communications director for Republican presidents Nixon, Ford, and Reagan and a campaign advisor to Clinton's 1992 opponent, George H. W. Bush.

At the time the president was coping with the fallout from two serious blunders: "Travelgate"—the badly managed shake-up of the White House Travel Office—and the Waco Seige—the disastrous federal assault on the Branch Davidian cult compound that ended in the death of eighty men, women, and children. Gergen would serve the president until late 1994. "For me," Gergen would later comment, "who had come from Republican administrations, which are very buttoned up, very hierarchical, very orderly, it was stunning. I mean I realize the Democrats are different in some ways. They like a little chaos. They think it's more creative. And who's to say they're wrong."

Photograph by J. Scott Applewhite

Reducing the Deficit

400

350

Inherited Deficit

300

Deficit With Clinton Budget

00

50

1993   1994   1995   1996   1997   1998

es: CBO

DEFICIT BUSTER: At the White House in June 1993, Bill Clinton sells his deficit reduction plan to the press. When President Ronald Reagan gradually reduced the top federal income tax rate from seventy percent to twenty-eight percent, the US debt began to soar. President George H. W. Bush raised the top rate slightly, to 31 percent in 1991—breaking a campaign promise and paying the price in the 1992 election—but the net result over twelve years of Republican rule was a quadrupling of the national debt from just under one trillion dollars to just over four trillion dollars.

During his eight years in office, Clinton would also increase the national debt—but by less than 50 percent—and according to the Congressional Budget Office, he actually presided over a budget surplus during his last four fiscal years in office—the first federal surplus in thirty years and the last since.

We're getting a lot more mail than any president ever has. By the time we had been here three-and-a-half months, more letters had come to the White House than in all of 1992.

—Bill Clinton to student volunteers,
June 12, 1993

CONNECTING: President Clinton shakes hands and trades hugs with more than 800 DC-area high school students on the steps of the Old Executive Office Building (now the Eisenhower Executive Office Building) on June 12, 1993. Clinton held the event to thank the students for their help opening the more than 3 million pieces of mail that the White House received during Clinton's first five months in office. The growing flood of correspondence may have reflected a public perception that Clinton was an empathetic chief executive who understood the lives of ordinary people.

RETALIATION: When US intelligence uncovered an Iraqi plot to assassinate former president George H. W. Bush with a car bomb during Bush's April 1993 visit to Kuwait, Clinton ordered a military response. Initially, the president wanted to target Iraqi leader Saddam Hussein directly, but Joint Chiefs of Staff Chairman Colin Powell convinced Clinton that bombing presidential palaces would probably miss Saddam and kill innocent civilians. General Powell suggested a more appropriate target—the Iraqi Intelligence Service headquarters—and Clinton agreed.

On June 26, 1993, two American naval vessels—one in the Persian Gulf and one in the Red Sea—fired twenty-three Tomahawk cruise missiles at the multi-building intelligence complex in central Baghdad. Most of the computer-guided missiles hit their target, but three landed in an upscale Baghdad neighborhood, killing eight civilians. In his Oval Office speech that evening, Clinton said he wanted to send three messages to the Iraqi leader: "We will combat terrorism. We will deter aggression. We will protect our people."

Photograph by Wilfredo Lee

COMMANDER-IN-CHIEF: Clinton got off to a rocky start with the military. His opponents branded him as a draft dodger during the 1992 presidential campaign. Then, within days of his inauguration, he initiated a controversial plan to end the ban on gays serving in the military. When the Joint Chiefs of Staff urged him to rethink this particular campaign promise, the apparent mutiny stirred a nationwide backlash against the plan. On July 19, 1993, Clinton announced his compromise solution—"Don't Ask, Don't Tell"—a clumsy policy that permitted gays to serve in the armed forces, provided they didn't tell anyone they were gay. "Don't Ask, Don't Tell" would remain in effect for the next eighteen years.

A week before his "Don't Ask, Don't Tell" announcement, Clinton, **above**, dines with officers at Pearl Harbor Naval Base in Hawaii after a Far East trip that included a G7 summit meeting of seven large-economy nations in Tokyo and a visit to US troops guarding the Demilitarized Zone between North and South Korea, **left**.

MUSICAL INTERLUDE: At a star-studded June 1993 White House concert celebrating the fortieth anniversary of the Newport Jazz Festival, the saxophonist-in-chief jams with jazz greats, **l–r** Jean-Baptiste "Illinois" Jacquet and Joshua Redman on tenor sax, and Robert "Red Rodney" Chudnick on trumpet. Redman, a summa cum laude graduate of Harvard, took the road the president didn't. Accepted at Clinton's alma mater, Yale Law School, he became a professional jazz musician instead.

HIS THIRD STEPFATHER: In 1981, three-time widow Virginia Cassidy Blythe Clinton Dwire married her fourth and last husband, food broker and longtime friend Dick Kelley. Here, the president visits the couple and their dog, Champ, in Hot Springs, Arkansas, during the summer of 1993. Six months later, Virginia, seventy, would die from breast cancer. Kelley, on the other hand, would reach the ripe old age of ninety-one. "I would come to love Dick Kelley and grow ever more grateful for the happiness he brought Mother and me," Clinton wrote later of his stepfather and occasional golf partner.

BUDGET BATTLE VICTORY: To reduce the burgeoning budget deficit he inherited from two Republican administrations—and armed with majorities in both houses of Congress—Clinton announced his intention to raise taxes. His legislation, popularly known as the Deficit Reduction Act of 1993, would lift the top incremental income tax rate in the United States from twenty-eight percent under Ronald Reagan and thirty-one percent under George H. W. Bush to 39.6 percent. Passage of the legislation was far from certain, and in the end, not one Republican—and not every Democrat—voted for the measure. The bill squeaked through the House 218–216. Then Vice President Al Gore, in his capacity as Senate President, broke a fifty-fifty tie in the Senate.

After the Senate vote, Republican Phil Gramm of Texas, declared: "I believe this program is going to make the economy weak. I believe hundreds of thousands of people are going to lose their jobs. I believe Bill Clinton will be one of those people." Gramm was wrong on all counts. The economy remained strong, unemployment dropped from 6.9 percent in 1993 to four percent in 2000, and Clinton kept his job for seven more years. The same couldn't be said for a significant number of Democratic lawmakers who supported the bill. They were voted out of office in the 1994 mid-term elections.

Clinton and his advisors, **left**, cluster around a tiny White House television to watch the House vote. Five days later, the president and vice president, **above**, stride onto the White House lawn to sign the measure into law.

The pope sure knew how to build a crowd. I just shook my head and said I'd hate to have to run against that man.

— BILL CLINTON, *My Life,* 2004

PAPAL GUIDANCE: On August 12, 1993, the president and his ambassador to the Holy See, former Boston mayor Raymond Flynn, **far right**, welcome Pope John Paul II to Stapleton International Airport in Denver. Clinton reported that his meeting with the pontiff was "productive," and that His Holiness supported US efforts in war-torn Somalia and Bosnia. The president and the pope disagreed on other issues, including abortion rights and population control, but after John Paul's 2005 funeral, Clinton would say, "Whether I agree or disagree with him, this guy is on my side. He cares about me as a human being—as a child of God. That's what made him great." The next day, the president signed the Colorado Wilderness Act, adding 612,000 acres of state and federally owned land to the National Wilderness Preservation System.

ADVICE FROM AL: The president and Al Gore, **above**, compare notes in the presidential limousine. Clinton and Gore—a second-generation Tennessee senator when Clinton tapped him for the vice presidency—met for lunch once a week throughout Clinton's presidency. "[He] helped me a lot in the early days," Clinton later wrote, "encouraging me to make the hard decisions and put them behind me, and giving me a continuing crash course in how Washington works."

REINVENTING GOVERNMENT: Two months into his administration, Clinton asked Al Gore to form an interagency task force that would streamline the federal government. At a September 7, 1993, news conference at the White House, **left**, Gore presents the National Performance Review's first report—384 specific recommendations that would collectively save $105 billion over five years. The stacked pallets of bureaucratic shelf-filler surrounding Bush and Gore represent the thousands of rules and regulations that the NPR wanted to ditch.

Gore's report made the *New York Times* best-seller list and was one of the first government documents posted on the Internet. In the end, Gore did much more than prepare a report. He led an effort that reduced the federal workforce by 100,000 employees and eliminated 26,000 pages of federal regulations. As Clinton later noted, the initiative "confounded our adversaries, elated our allies, and escaped the notice of most of the public because it was neither sensational nor controversial."

Photographs by Robert McNeely

PEACE BROKER: At the White House on September 13, 1993, President Clinton and Vice President Gore meet with Israeli Premier Yitzhak Rabin and Foreign Minister Shimon Peres just before Rabin signs the Declaration of Principles on Interim Self-Government Arrangements. The agreement—more commonly known as the Oslo Accords—was secretly negotiated at the Fafo Institute in Oslo, Norway during the first-ever face-to-face talks between Israel and the Palestinian Liberation Organization. These negotiations also produced Letters of Mutual Recognition in which the PLO acknowledged for the first time the existence of the state of Israel and pledged to reject violence, and Israel first recognized the PLO as the official Palestinian authority.

The Oslo Accords called for the withdrawal of Israeli troops from certain parts of the West Bank and the Gaza Strip and affirmed the Palestinians' right to self-government, but it purposely kicked several thorny issues down the road—including the status of Jerusalem, the right of return for Palestinian refugees, and Israeli settlements in the Occupied Territories.

Photograph by Robert McNeely

HANDSHAKE INSTEAD OF A HUG: Clinton presides over the historic handshake between Israeli Prime Minister Yitzhak Rabin and PLO Chairman Yasser Arafat after they signed the Oslo Accords on the South Lawn of the White House. At the time, many Israelis still regarded the PLO leader as an unrepentant terrorist, so Rabin—who would be assassinated by a right-wing Israeli zealot two years later—took a real political risk simply by shaking hands with Arafat. The prime minister wanted to make sure that a handshake was as far as it went and that Arafat did not try to embrace him Palestinian-style. Rabin and Clinton, who were very close, discussed the issue ahead of the ceremony. They decided that Clinton would station himself between the two leaders and intervene if Arafat drew in for a hug. The resulting visual—Clinton, arms outstretched, bringing the warring parties together while Rabin keeps his distance—worked for both the US and Israeli electorates.

Photograph by Vince Musi

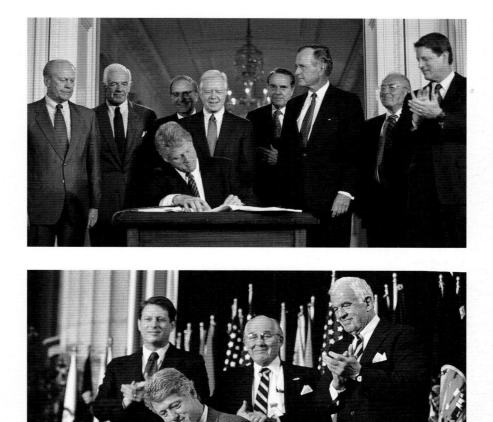

BI-PARTISAN EFFORT: President Clinton and former presidents George Bush, Jimmy Carter, and Gerald Ford, **left**, walk past Aaron Shikler's posthumous portrait of John F. Kennedy en route to a September 1993 White House press conference kicking off the bipartisan campaign to ratify the North American Free Trade Accord. Initiated by the first Bush administration, the proposed NAFTA trade pact between the United States, Canada, and Mexico would eliminate virtually all tariffs and trade restrictions between the three nations, creating the world's largest free-trade zone. The measure, which garnered more Republican than Democratic votes in both houses of Congress, would pass later that year, but only after Clinton added more safeguards for American workers and stronger environmental restrictions.

NAFTA's effects have been debated ever since, but when Clinton signed the bill in 1993, he took the long view: "We are on the verge of a global economic expansion that is sparked by the fact that the United States, at this critical moment, decided that we would compete, not retreat." **Top**: The NAFTA kickoff. **Bottom**: Clinton signs the NAFTA legislation into law on December 8, 1993.

Photograph by Robert McNeely (left)

Sargent Shriver, the first director of the Peace Corps, lent me one of the pens that President Kennedy had used thirty-two years earlier to sign the Peace Corps legislation, and I used it to bring AmeriCorps into being.

—BILL CLINTON, *My Life*, 2004

A PROMISE KEPT: One of Clinton's signature campaign promises was the creation of a national volunteer service agency similar to the Peace Corps, but with a domestic focus. On September 21, 1993, flanked by, **l–r**, senior White House aide Eli Segal, Senator Ted Kennedy, Vice President Al Gore, and a group of student volunteers, President Clinton signed the National and Community Service Trust Act into law. The legislation combined several federal and community service programs plus the new AmeriCorps program into the Corporation for National and Community Service.

In its first five years, AmeriCorps deployed nearly 200,000 young Americans across the country to assist communities with education, public safety, health, and environmental initiatives. Eli Segal, who was chief of staff of Clinton's 1992 presidential campaign, helped shepherd the legislation through Congress and became the nonprofit corporation's first chief executive. In his second term, Clinton would ask Segal to head the Welfare to Work Partnership, where he encouraged American businesses to hire welfare recipients.

LAST-MINUTE CHANGES: Bill Clinton promised comprehensive health care legislation during the first hundred days of his presidency. Eight months later—on September 22, 1993—he finally presented his reform package to a joint session of Congress. The highly complex 1,300-page plan—formulated by Hillary Rodham Clinton's Task Force on National Health Care in consultation with literally thousands of stakeholders—promised comprehensive health coverage for all Americans and generated intense opposition from entrenched interests. Bill and Hillary, **above**, were still tweaking the president's address during their limousine ride from the White House to Capitol Hill.

Photograph by Robert McNeely

TEAM EFFORT: The president—whose memory is legendary—had a strong grasp of the health care legislation. After motioning the assembled senators and representatives to sit down, Clinton, **above**, began to read what he thought would be his health care address, only to find that his staff had loaded the wrong speech into the Teleprompter. Unfazed, he recited the health care address by heart, winging it for seven minutes until the problem was finally fixed. Not even Hillary—who sat in the balcony with celebrity pediatrician T. Berry Brazelton and Ronald Reagan's surgeon general, C. Everett Koop—realized there was a problem.

A week later, Hillary, **facing page**, **bottom**, was back on Capitol Hill, in the extraordinary role of lead testifier before five congressional committees. "I'm here as a mother, a wife, a daughter, a sister, a woman," she began. By all accounts, she did a masterful job, answering complex questions without notes for hours. After the launch, the First Couple set out across the country to sell the plan to voters.

But entrenched forces were arrayed against them—including the Republican leadership and the powerful insurance industry, which launched its famously effective "Harry and Louise" advertising campaign. Combined with the Clintons' own missteps and breaking crises in Somalia, Russia, and the Balkans that pulled the administration's attention overseas, these forces would slow and finally kill significant health care reform for nearly two decades

BLACK HAWK DOWN: Among the front-burner issues Clinton inherited from the Bush administration was a nasty conflict in starving, chaotic Somalia, where 4,000 US soldiers supported 22,000 UN peacekeepers. In an effort to capture two top lieutenants of renegade warlord Mohamed Ali Farrah Aidid, the president signed off on an Army Ranger–Delta Force raid on Aidid's central Mogadishu headquarters.

The mission went badly from the start: two US Black Hawk helicopters were shot down with rocket-propelled grenades, then surrounded by an armed mob numbering in the thousands. All hell broke loose during the massive effort to rescue the downed pilots and crew (later depicted in the popular 2001 film *Black Hawk Down*). Hundreds of Somalis and nineteen Americans were killed in the vicious firefight that lasted through the night and into the next day. Images of dead American soldiers, dragged through the streets of Mogadishu, stunned the nation and eventually led to the withdrawal of American forces. The Black Hawk Down Incident also colored Clinton's decision not to intervene during the 1994 Rwanda genocide—a choice he later regretted. Clinton, his military advisors, and members of his foreign policy team, **above**, study a surveillance map of Somalia on October 5, 1993, the day after the Battle of Mogadishu.

Photograph by Robert McNeely (above)

PHONE CALL FROM A FRIEND: Still reeling from the bloody events in Somalia, Clinton offers an ear to the Russian Federation's pro-Western president, Boris Yeltsin, while flying to California aboard Air Force One. At the time, Yeltsin was confronting a constitutional crisis.

On September 21, after months of conflict, the Russian leader tried to illegally dissolve the Russian parliament. The parliament, in turn, tried to impeach Yeltsin. In the weeks that followed, anti-Yeltsin street mobs—activated by Russia's failing economy and egged on by rebellious parliamentarians—attacked Moscow's television broadcast center and the mayor's office, while rebel leaders barricaded themselves in the White House—the massive Soviet-era edifice that housed the parliament. On October 4—the day before this photograph was taken—Yeltsin directed loyal elements of the Russian army to encircle the White House with ten tanks that fired shells at the upper floors. Then loyalist troops took the building, floor by floor. It was Moscow's bloodiest episode since the 1917 revolution—and along with the Black Hawk Down incident, it drew the administration's—and the nation's—attention away from Hillary Clinton's attempt to build support for her health care initiative.

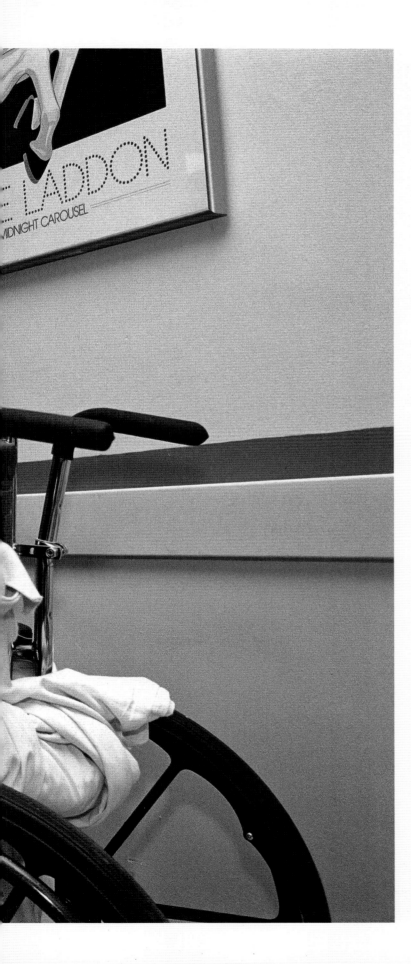

A COMPLICATED MAN: Bill Clinton's skills as a retail politician may be unparalleled. Veteran Arkansas newspaperman Ernest Dumas ascribed the president's political success to his prodigious memory: "He never forgets anyone. Never." Another factor is the immense—and sincere—natural empathy that Clinton inherited from his mother. The president, **left**, connects with a young patient in the pediatric ward of the Robert Wood Johnson University Hospital in New Brunswick, New Jersey, on October 8, 1993. Another Clinton inheritance was his biological father's eye for the ladies. **Above**, the forty-third president appreciates Giambologna's sixteenth-century Cesarini Venus at the US Embassy in Rome in June 1994.

Photograph by Robert McNeely (above)

GUNS: President Clinton, **above**, signs the Brady Handgun Violence Prevention Act into law on November 30, 1993. At his side is former White House press secretary James Brady, who suffered a debilitating wound to the head during John Hinckley's 1981 attempt on President Ronald Reagan's life. Hinckley, the would-be assassin, had a history of psychiatric problems and a gun-related arrest, but he was still able to purchase a .22-caliber revolver and exploding Devastator bullets at a Texas pawnshop. For more than a decade, Brady and his wife, Sarah, spearheaded a campaign to require background checks for handgun buyers. Clinton later claimed that the Brady Bill prevented more than 600,000 felons, fugitives, and stalkers from buying handguns during his administration alone. A year after the bill became law, the National Rifle Association helped defeat many of the lawmakers who supported it.

AND BUTTER: The president, **left**, enjoys what a British newspaper called "rip-roaring political entertainment"—a NAFTA debate between Vice President Al Gore and Clinton's 1992 opponent, Ross Perot, on CNN's popular *Larry King Live*. The next morning, *USA Today* declared Gore the hands-down winner, and public support for NAFTA soared. "We're going to win this thing," Clinton predicted, and despite Perot's warning about a "giant sucking sound" as US jobs migrated to cheaper labor markets south of the border, NAFTA passed both houses of Congress with strong Republican and some Democratic support.

ECONOMIC ADVISORS: President Clinton meets with, **l–r**, Federal Reserve Chairman Alan Greenspan, Treasury Secretary and former Texas senator Lloyd Bentsen, the chairman of the newly created National Economic Council and former co-chair of Goldman Sachs, Robert Rubin, and Vice President Al Gore. Their agenda: reduce the $300 billion federal budget deficit; lower interest rates; spur private investment; invest in science, job training, education, and research; and open foreign markets to American goods. Over the eight-year course of the Clinton administration, they would be largely successful.

Photograph by Robert McNeely

CABINET SECRETARIES: Presidential advisor George Stephanopoulos grabs the president's ear during a cabinet meeting. To Clinton's right, Secretary of State Warren Christopher; to his left, Defense Secretary Les Aspin and Commerce Secretary Ron Brown. Christopher served until the end of Clinton's first term and was succeeded by UN ambassador Madeleine Albright, who became America's first female Secretary of State. Defense Secretary Aspin, in poor health and dogged by the Black Hawk Down and "Don't Ask, Don't Tell" debacles, resigned after a year, replaced by his deputy, William Perry. In 1995, Aspin would die at age fifty-six from a congenital heart condition. Ron Brown, the well-liked former chairman of the Democratic National Committee, would also die young. He and thirty-four others were killed in a plane crash during a US trade mission to the Balkans in April 1996. "I was devastated," Clinton wrote later of Brown's death. "Ron was my friend and my best political advisor in the cabinet."

Photograph by Robert McNeely

GOOD-BYE, VIRGINIA: "No church wa[s] friends and it was too cold to hold the fu[neral] racetrack, so we scheduled it for the Con[ ] his memoir. Here, on January 8, 1994, C[ ] half-brother, Roger, as they leave Virginia['s] back from a glamorous Las Vegas jaunt wh[ ] bra Streisand, Virginia passed away from [ ] her own bed. Immediately after his moth[er] dent flew to Brussels, where he hoped to [ ] Europe into the NATO alliance. As Clin[ton] but not for very long."

Photograph by Doug Mills

THE SHOW GOES ON: Six days after his mother's burial, Clinton plays for his supper at Russian President Boris Yeltsin's dacha near Moscow. Clinton's saxophone was a gift from Yeltsin—one of at least six the president received during his presidential tenure. Clinton and Yeltsin's friendship was both authentic and strategic. Clinton needed a stable, liberalized Russia to expand the NATO alliance, and Yeltsin needed US support to backstop his reformist domestic agenda and fend off challenges from Russia's revanchist right wing.

Photograph by Robert McNeely

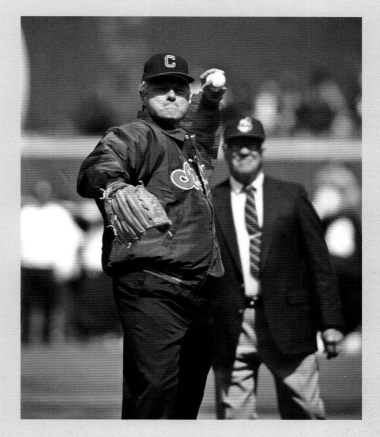

PLAY BALL: On April 4, 1994, the president, **above**, throws out the first pitch on Opening Day at Cleveland's brand-new Jacobs Field. The president had a lot a riding on this pitch. The previous year, he became the first president in history to successfully throw an Opening Day pitch from the center of the mound to home plate. So Bill drafted Chelsea, fourteen, to catch practice pitches in the Rose Garden, **left**, the day before his Major League appearance.

Bill and Chelsea maintained a close relationship that would weather several storms in the years ahead. Although there were obvious drawbacks to raising an only child in the White House, Bill would later observe that Chelsea benefited from the fact that her parents both lived and worked in the same building.

I've always believed in a zone of privacy.... After resisting that for a long time, I've been rezoned.

—Hillary Clinton, April 22, 1994

WHITEWATER: On January 20, 1994, the administration's one-year anniversary, Attorney General Janet Reno appointed former US Attorney Robert Fiske, a moderate Republican, to investigate Bill and Hillary's role in a money-losing Arkansas real estate development called Whitewater Estates.

Because the Watergate-era law regarding independent counsels had lapsed, no special prosecutor could be appointed unless President Clinton specifically requested the investigation. White House Counsel Bernard Nussbaum argued strenuously against that course of action, warning the president that an independent counsel with a limitless budget, unbounded scope of inquiry, and an open time frame would search for some sort of wrongdoing for the remainder of Clinton's presidency. In retrospect, the president would agree wholeheartedly, but in 1994 he thought that he had nothing to hide and that resisting the probe would make him look guilty. "At the time," Hillary Clinton later wrote, "Whitewater seemed to me like…more of a nuisance than a threat."

The *New York Times* first raised the Whitewater controversy during the 1992 presidential campaign. The story faded until October 1993, when the Resolution Trust Corporation launched a criminal investigation of the Clintons'

Whitewater partner, Jim McDougal, for looting a failed Arkansas-based savings and loan. Later, when reporters learned that Hillary's chief of staff had removed Whitewater documents from Vince Foster's office following the deputy White House counsel's 1993 suicide, the story took a conspiratorial turn, and conservative talk radio crackled with far-fetched theories about murder and cover-ups.

On April 22, 1994, Hillary Clinton, **facing page**, decided to face Whitewater head on at what came to be called the "Pretty in Pink" press conference. Dressed in a pink sweater set, Hillary gamely answered endless questions about Whitewater minutiae and her 1979 commodities windfall, but her candor did little to dampen the story. Three months later, a panel of three conservative judges appointed by Chief Justice William Rehnquist would replace independent counsel Robert Fiske with right-wing zealot Kenneth Starr, who would embark on a six-year, $70 million witch hunt that ended with the Clintons' exoneration on all Whitewater charges and the president's impeachment on an entirely unrelated matter—just as Bernie Nussbaum predicted.

Photograph by Doug Mills

THE HELP: "Clinton's anger was an impersonal physical force, like a tornado," wrote presidential advisor George Stephanopoulos in his memoir, *All Too Human*. "The tantrum would form in an instant and exhaust itself in a violent rush. Whoever happened to be in the way would have to deal with it; more often than not, that person was me." The president, **above**, screams at Stephanopoulos outside the Oval Office while senior advisor David Gergen looks on. On another occasion, **facing page**, **top**, Senior Advisor Rahm Emanuel (later Barack Obama's chief of staff) feels the presidential love.

Photographs by Robert McNeely (above and facing page, top)

EMPLOYEE RELATIONS: In late 1995, the US government shut down twice while the president and Newt Gingrich's Republican-controlled House played chicken over the federal budget. Nearly 800,000 federal workers were sent home, including many White House staffers. Volunteers—including a fresh-faced twenty-two-year-old intern from Beverly Hills named Monica Lewinsky, **left**—took up the slack. Lewinsky, who originally interned for White House Chief of Staff Leon Panetta, snagged a paid position in the White House Office of Legislative Affairs in December 1995. She worked there for four months before moving to the Pentagon—a relocation engineered by White House staffers who suspected an inappropriate relationship with the president. The plan backfired when Lewinsky confided in Pentagon staffer Linda Tripp, who secretly recorded their conversations.

PRELUDE TO PEACE: On July 25, 1994, President Clinton plays notary as Jordan's King Hussein bin Talal and Israel's Prime Minister Yitzhak Rabin sign the Washington Declaration, which formally ended the forty-six-year state of war between Israel and the Hashemite Kingdom of Jordan. Three months later, Clinton and Secretary of State Warren Christopher would travel to the Israel–Jordan border, north of Eilat, to witness the formal signing.

Photograph by David Rubinger

CRIME AND PUNISHMENT: "We were working on crime through good-faith bipartisan negotiation," Clinton noted proudly in his memoir. The Violent Crime Control and Law Enforcement Act of 1994—hashed out between congressional Democrats and Republicans—was signed into law by the president on September 13, 1994. Included in the legislation were a ban on certain assault weapons, tougher penalties for repeat offenders, expansion of federal crimes subject to the death penalty, funding for 100,000 new community police officers, increased prison funding, and prevention programs aimed at keeping kids out of trouble. Although the contributing factors are widely debated, over the next two decades violent crime in the United States would drop nearly 50 percent from its early 1990s peak.

REPUBLICAN REVOLUTION: With stunning decisiveness, Republicans swept the 1994 midterm elections, winning control of both the House and Senate for the first time in forty years. Republicans also added twenty state legislatures and twelve governorships to their column. Although incumbent presidents normally lose congressional seats during midterm elections, the scope of the 1994 defeat was unprecedented. "On November 8, we got the living daylights beat out of us," Clinton later wrote.

Popular Republican initiatives and a drumbeat of White House missteps led to the walloping. Minority Whip Newt Gingrich's bold "Contract with America"—an ambitious list of promises that included a balanced budget, tougher criminal penalties, welfare cuts, tort reform, and congressional term limits—struck a chord with voters. The White House, on the other hand, appeared to be stumbling from one crisis to the next—most notably, Travelgate, Filegate, Whitewater, "Don't Ask, Don't Tell," Vince Foster's suicide, and the collapse of Hillary Clinton's health care initiative.

Clinton's midterm thrashing would have several consequences, some unexpected: Hillary Clinton would become a somewhat more conventional first lady, focusing more on women's and children's issues. Republicans would eventually overplay their hand and alienate the voters who elected them. Bill Clinton would quietly bring bare-knuckled Republican pollster Dick Morris, who helped him regain the Arkansas governorship, back into the fold. And Clinton, whose chances of reelection seemed to be slim to none in 1994, would pick himself up and begin one of his more prolific periods of legislative success.

On December 2, 1994, the president and vice president, **above**, met at the White House with the new Senate majority leader, Bob Dole, and the new speaker of the House, firebrand Georgia congressman Newt Gingrich. **Facing page**: Even after his midterm drubbing, Clinton, had at least one loyal companion—Socks the cat.

TERRORISM STRIKES HOME: At 9 a.m. on Wednesday, April 19, 1995, a massive car bomb destroyed much of the Alfred P. Murrah Federal Office Building in downtown Oklahoma City. The blast killed 168 people and wounded another 680. Within an hour of the explosion, police stopped Timothy McVeigh, a fan of the American militia movement, for driving without a license plate and arrested him for carrying a concealed weapon. Evidence in McVeigh's car linked him to the bombing and ended rush-to-judgment speculation that the attack had been carried out by Islamic militants.

McVeigh chose the day of his attack to mark the one-year anniversary of the deadly FBI raid on the Branch Davidian compound in Waco, Texas—an event that came to symbolize big-government tyranny among some right-wing extremists. On the following Sunday, April 23, the president and first lady attended a memorial service at the Oklahoma State Fairgrounds. They also received a briefing **above**, from search-and-rescue teams who were still scrambling to find survivors in the rubble. Clinton's speech that day, considered a masterpiece of American rhetoric, comforted a grieving nation and burnished Clinton's presidential image

OKLAHOMA CITY BOMBING MEMORIAL PRAYER SERVICE ADDRESS

Bill Clinton, April 23, 1995

Thank you very much, Governor Keating and Mrs. Keating,[1] Reverend Graham,[2] to the families of those who have been lost and wounded, to the people of Oklahoma City, who have endured so much, and the people of this wonderful state, to all of you who are here as our fellow Americans.

I am honored to be here today to represent the American people. But I have to tell you that Hillary and I also come as parents, as husband and wife, as people who were your neighbors for some of the best years of our lives.

Today our nation joins with you in grief. We mourn with you. We share your hope against hope that some may still survive. We thank all those who have worked so heroically to save lives and to solve this crime—those here in Oklahoma and those who are all across this great land, and many who left their own lives to come here to work hand in hand with you. We pledge to do all we can to help you heal the injured, to rebuild this city, and to bring to justice those who did this evil.

[1] Frank Keating served as the twenty-fifth governor of Oklahoma from 1995 until 2003. His wife, Cathy, made an unsuccessful bid for one of Oklahoma's five congressional seats in 2001.

[2] A Christian evangelist who advised American presidents beginning with Harry Truman.

This terrible sin took the lives of our American family: innocent children[3] in that building only because their parents were trying to be good parents as well as good workers; citizens in the building going about their daily business; and many there who served the rest of us—who worked to help the elderly and the disabled, who worked to support our farmers and our veterans, who worked to enforce our laws and to protect us. Let us say clearly, they served us well, and we are grateful.

But for so many of you they were also neighbors and friends. You saw them at church or the PTA meetings, at the civic clubs, at the ballpark. You know them in ways that all the rest of America could not. And to all the members of the families here present who have suffered loss, though we share your grief, your pain is unimaginable, and we know that. We cannot undo it. That is God's work.

We pledge to do all we can to help you heal the injured, to rebuild this city, and to bring to justice those who did this evil.

Our words seem small beside the loss you have endured. But I found a few I wanted to share today. I've received a lot of letters in these last terrible days. One stood out because it came from a young widow and a mother of three whose own husband was murdered with more than two hundred other Americans when Pan Am 103 was shot down. Here is what that woman said I should say to you today:

The anger you feel is valid, but you must not allow yourselves to be consumed by it. The hurt you feel must not be allowed to turn into hate, but instead into the search for justice. The loss you feel must not paralyze your own lives. Instead, you must try to pay tribute to your loved ones by continuing to do all the things they left undone, thus ensuring they did not die in vain.

Wise words from one who also knows.

You have lost too much, but you have not lost everything. And you have certainly not lost America, for we will stand with you for as many tomorrows as it takes.

If ever we needed evidence of that, I could only recall the words of Governor and Mrs. Keating: "If anybody thinks that Americans are mostly mean and selfish, they ought to come to Oklahoma. If anybody thinks Americans have lost the capacity for love and caring and courage, they ought to come to Oklahoma."

To all my fellow Americans beyond this hall, I say, one thing we owe those who have

---

[3] Nineteen children under the age of six in the building's day care center were killed by the blast.

sacrificed is the duty to purge ourselves of the dark forces which gave rise to this evil. They are forces that threaten our common peace, our freedom, our way of life. Let us teach our children that the God of comfort is also the God of righteousness: Those who trouble their own house will inherit the wind. Justice will prevail.

Let us let our own children know that we will stand against the forces of fear. When there is talk of hatred, let us stand up and talk against it. When there is talk of violence, let us stand up and talk against it. In the face of death, let us honor life. As Saint Paul admonished us, let us "not be overcome by evil, but overcome evil with good."

Yesterday, Hillary and I had the privilege of speaking with some children of other federal employees—children like those who were lost here. And one little girl said something we will never forget. She said, "We should all plant a tree in memory of the children." So this morning before we got on the plane to come here, at the White House, we planted that tree in honor of the children of Oklahoma. It was a dogwood with its wonderful spring flower and its deep, enduring roots. It embodies the lesson of the Psalms that the life of a good person is like a tree whose leaf does not wither.

My fellow Americans, a tree takes a long time to grow and wounds take a long time to heal. But we must begin. Those who are lost now belong to God. Some day we will be with them. But until that happens, their legacy must be our lives.

Thank you all, and God bless you.

THE TIES THAT BIND: To further clarify the nature of Palestinian self-government in the Israeli-occupied West Bank and Gaza, Israeli Prime Minister Yitzhak Rabin and PLO Chairman Yasir Arafat signed the Israeli-Palestinian Interim Agreement—also known as Oslo II—in Washington on September 28, 1995. Adjusting their neckwear before the White House ceremony are, **above**, l–r, Rabin, Egyptian President Hosni Mubarak, King Hussein of Jordan, Clinton, and Arafat—who preferred a scarf. The risk Rabin took by granting Palestinians a further measure of autonomy would soon become apparent. Only a month after this photo was taken, Yigal Amir, a radical right-wing Israeli law student, would assassinate Rabin after a pro–Oslo Accords rally in Tel Aviv.

RADIO DAYS: The president, **right**, prepares for his weekly radio address from the Oval Office. Franklin Roosevelt began the practice of periodic radio addresses in 1933 with his "fireside chats." President Reagan revived the tradition in 1982. Clinton's successor, George W. Bush, would modernize the practice, distributing podcasts of his address, and President Barack Obama would add a video version on the White House website and YouTube.

IRON MEN: Camden Yards sold out the night that Baltimore Orioles shortstop Cal Ripken Jr. broke Lou Gehrig's half-century-old record for consecutive games played. On September 6, 1995, Ripken completed his 2,131st consecutive game—and hit a home run to boot. Among those in the stands were Ripken's father, Al Gore, and the president, **above**, who received a signed bat after the game.

CROSSWORD GEEK: Bill Clinton settles into the *New York Times* crossword puzzle aboard the presidential helicopter, Marine One, on October 15, 1995. A renowned multitasker, Clinton sometimes did crosswords during White House meetings, disconcerting other participants until they realized that Clinton still heard and understood everything said—with brainpower left over. In an interview for the 2006 documentary *Wordplay*, Clinton compared his crossword strategy to his presidential style. In both cases, he said, "You start with what you know the answers to, and you just build on it. Eventually, you can unravel the whole puzzle."

Photograph by Robert McNeely (right)

WOMEN'S RIGHTS: As honorary chairwoman of the US delegation to the UN Fourth World Conference on Women in Beijing, Hillary Clinton speaks at a women's health colloquium. Later that day, she gave another, more important speech to the conference's plenary session. The occasion was fraught with political peril. Hillary could offend either her Chinese hosts, who were sensitive to a raft of human rights issues, or her conservative critics, who had already complained that the conference was, in biographer Carl Bernstein's words, "shaping up as an unsanctioned festival of anti-family, anti-American sentiment."

While preparing her speech, an aide asked what she wanted to accomplish. Hillary answered, "I want to push the envelope as far as I can on behalf of women and girls." In the end, the first lady's speech—reprinted on the following pages—inspired a standing ovation and worldwide coverage. Hillary's impulse to make a difference in the lives of women and children—first manifested at Yale Law School—had finally been realized. A *New York Times* editorial the next day called Hillary's speech "her finest moment in public life."

Photograph by Doug Mills

REMARKS TO THE PLENARY SESSION OF THE UN FOURTH WORLD CONFERENCE ON WOMEN

Hillary Rodham Clinton, Beijing, September 5, 1995

I would like to thank the Secretary General for inviting me to be part of this important United Nations Fourth World Conference on Women. This is truly a celebration—a celebration of the contributions women make in every aspect of life: in the home, on the job, in the community, as mothers, wives, sisters, daughters, learners, workers, citizens, and leaders.

It is also a coming together, much the way women come together every day in every country. We come together in fields and factories, in village markets and supermarkets, in living rooms and boardrooms. Whether it is while playing with our children in the park, or washing clothes in a river, or taking a break at the office water cooler, we come together and talk about our aspirations and concerns. And time and again, our talk turns to our children and our families. However different we may appear, there is far more that unites us than divides us. We share a common future, and we are here to find common ground so that we may help bring new dignity and respect to women and girls all over the world, and in so doing bring new strength and stability to families as well.

By gathering in Beijing, we are focusing world attention on issues that matter most in our lives—the lives of women and their families: access to education, health care, jobs and credit, the chance to enjoy basic legal and human rights and to participate fully in the political life of our countries.

There are some who question the reason for this conference. Let them listen to the voices of women in their homes, neighborhoods, and workplaces. There are some who wonder whether the lives of women and girls matter to economic and political progress around the globe. Let them look at the women gathered here and at Huairou[1]—the homemakers and nurses, the teachers and lawyers, the policymakers, and women who run their own businesses. It is conferences like this that compel governments and peoples everywhere to listen, look, and face the world's most pressing problems. Wasn't it, after all, after the women's conference in Nairobi ten years ago that the world focused for the first time on the crisis of domestic violence?

Earlier today, I participated in a World Health Organization forum. In that forum, we talked about ways that government officials, NGOs, and individual citizens are working to address the health problems of women and girls. Tomorrow, I will attend a gathering of the United Nations Development Fund for Women. There, the discussion will focus on local—and highly successful—programs that give hardworking women access to credit so they can improve their own lives and the lives of their families.

What we are learning around the world is that if women are healthy and educated, their families will flourish. If women are free from violence, their families will flourish. If women have a chance to work and earn as full and equal partners in society, their families will flourish. And when families flourish, communities and nations do as well. That is why every woman, every man, every child, every family, and every nation on this planet does have a stake in the discussion that takes place here.

Over the past twenty-five years, I have worked persistently on issues relating to women, children, and families. Over the past two and a half years, I've had the opportunity to learn more about the challenges facing women in my own country and around the world. I have met new mothers in Indonesia, who come together regularly in their village to discuss nutrition, family planning, and baby care. I have met working parents in Denmark who talk about the comfort they feel in knowing that their children can be cared for in safe and nurturing after-school centers. I have met women in South Africa who helped lead the struggle to end apartheid and are now helping to build a new democracy. I have met with the leading women of my own hemisphere who are working every day to promote literacy and better health care for children in their countries. I have met women in India and Bangladesh who are taking out small loans to buy milk cows, or rickshaws, or thread in order to create a livelihood for themselves and their families. I have met the doctors and nurses in Belarus and Ukraine who are trying to keep children alive in the aftermath of Chernobyl.[2]

---

[1] Concerned that representatives of nongovernmental organizations might criticize its human rights record, the Chinese government exiled the NGO portion of the conference to the small town of Huairou, thirty-five miles north of Beijing.

[2] In 1986, there was a devastating accident at the Chernobyl nuclear power plant in Ukraine.

The great challenge of this conference is to give voice to women everywhere whose experiences go unnoticed, whose words go unheard. Women comprise more than half the world's population, 70 percent of the world's poor, and two-thirds of those who are not taught to read and write. We are the primary caretakers for most of the world's children and elderly. Yet much of the work we do is not valued—not by economists, not by historians, not by popular culture, not by government leaders.

At this very moment, as we sit here, women around the world are giving birth, raising children, cooking meals, washing clothes, cleaning houses, planting crops, working on assembly lines, running companies, and running countries. Women also are dying from diseases that should have been prevented or treated. They are watching their children succumb to malnutrition caused by poverty and economic depriva-

Every woman deserves the chance to realize her own God-given potential.

tion. They are being denied the right to go to school by their own fathers and brothers. They are being forced into prostitution, and they are being barred from the bank lending offices and banned from the ballot box.

Those of us who have the opportunity to be here have the responsibility to speak for those who could not. As an American, I want to speak for women in my own country, women who are raising children on the minimum wage, women who can't afford health care or child care, women whose lives are threatened by violence, including violence in their own homes.

I want to speak up for mothers who are fighting for good schools, safe neighborhoods, clean air, and clean airwaves; for older women, some of them widows, who find that, after raising their families, their skills and life experiences are not valued in the marketplace; for women who are working all night as nurses, hotel clerks, or fast food chefs so that they can be at home during the day with their children; and for women everywhere who simply don't have time to do everything they are called upon to do each and every day.

Speaking to you today, I speak for them, just as each of us speaks for women around the world who are denied the chance to go to school, or see a doctor, or own property, or have a say about the direction of their lives, simply because they are women. The truth is that most women around the world work both inside and outside the home, usually by necessity.

We need to understand there is no one formula for how women should lead our lives. That is why we must respect the choices that each woman makes for herself and her family. Every woman deserves the chance to realize her own God-given potential. But we must recognize that women will never gain full dignity until their human rights are respected and protected.

Our goals for this conference, to strengthen families and societies by empowering women to take greater control over their own destinies, cannot be fully achieved unless all governments—here and around the world—accept their responsibility to protect and promote internationally recognized human rights. The international community has long acknowledged and recently reaffirmed at Vienna[3] that both women and men are entitled to a range of protections and personal freedoms, from the right of personal security to the right to determine freely the number and spacing of the children they bear. No one should be forced to remain silent for fear of religious or political persecution, arrest, abuse, or torture.

Tragically, women are most often the ones whose human rights are violated. Even now, in the late twentieth century, the rape of women continues to be used as an instrument of armed conflict. Women and children make up a large majority of the world's refugees. And when women are excluded from the political process, they become even more vulnerable to abuse. I believe that now, on the eve of a new millennium, it is time to break the silence. It is time for us to say here in Beijing, and for the world to hear, that it is no longer acceptable to discuss women's rights as separate from human rights.

These abuses have continued because, for too long, the history of women has been a history of silence. Even today, there are those who are trying to silence our words. But the voices of this conference and of the women at Huairou must be heard loudly and clearly[4]:

It is a violation of human rights when babies are denied food, or drowned, or suffocated, or their spines broken, simply because they are born girls.

It is a violation of human rights when women and girls are sold into the slavery of prostitution for human greed—and the kinds of reasons that are used to justify this practice should no longer be tolerated.

It is a violation of human rights when women are doused with gasoline, set on fire, and burned to death because their marriage dowries are deemed too small.

It is a violation of human rights when individual women are raped in their own communities and when thousands of women are subjected to rape as a tactic or prize of war.

---

[3] Vienna was the site of the United Nations World Conference on Human Rights, held in June 1993. The resulting Vienna Declaration stated in part, "The human rights of women … are an inalienable, integral and indivisible part of universal human rights. The full and equal participation of women in political, civil, economic, social and cultural life, at the national, regional and international levels, and the eradication of all forms of discrimination on grounds of sex are priority objectives of the international community."

[4] A subtle gibe at the Chinese government for exiling the NGO portion of the conference to Huairou.

It is a violation of human rights when a leading cause of death worldwide among women ages fourteen to forty-four is the violence they are subjected to in their own homes by their own relatives.

It is a violation of human rights when young girls are brutalized by the painful and degrading practice of genital mutilation.

It is a violation of human rights when women are denied the right to plan their own families, and that includes being forced to have abortions or being sterilized against their will.

Human rights are women's rights and women's rights are human rights once and for all.

If there is one message that echoes forth from this conference, let it be that human rights are women's rights and women's rights are human rights once and for all. Let us not forget that among those rights are the right to speak freely—and the right to be heard.

Women must enjoy the rights to participate fully in the social and political lives of their countries, if we want freedom and democracy to thrive and endure. It is indefensible that many women in nongovernmental organizations who wished to participate in this conference have not been able to attend—or have been prohibited from fully taking part.

Let me be clear. Freedom means the right of people to assemble, organize, and debate openly. It means respecting the views of those who may disagree with the views of their governments. It means not taking citizens away from their loved ones and jailing them, mistreating them, or denying them their freedom or dignity because of the peaceful expression of their ideas and opinions.

In my country, we recently celebrated the seventy-fifth anniversary of women's suffrage. It took one hundred and fifty years after the signing of our Declaration of Independence for women to win the right to vote. It took seventy-two years of organized struggle, before that happened, on the part of many courageous women and men. It was one of America's most divisive philosophical wars. But it was a bloodless war. Suffrage was achieved without a shot being fired.

But we have also been reminded, in V-J Day observances last weekend,[5] of the good that comes when men and women join together to combat the forces of tyranny and to build a better world. We have seen peace prevail in most places for a half century. We have avoided another world war. But we have not solved older, deeply rooted problems that continue to diminish the potential of half the world's population.

Now it is the time to act on behalf of women everywhere. If we take bold steps to better the lives of women, we will be taking bold steps to better the lives of children and families too.

Families rely on mothers and wives for emotional support and care. Families rely on women for labor in the home. And increasingly, everywhere, families rely on women for income needed to raise healthy children and care for other relatives.

As long as discrimination and inequities remain so commonplace everywhere in the world, as long as girls and women are valued less, fed less, fed last, overworked, underpaid, not schooled, subjected to violence in and outside their homes—the potential of the human family to create a peaceful, prosperous world will not be realized.

Let this conference be our—and the world's—call to action. Let us heed that call so we can create a world in which every woman is treated with respect and dignity, every boy and girl is loved and cared for equally, and every family has the hope of a strong and stable future. That is the work before you. That is the work before all of us who have a vision of the world we want to see for our children and our grandchildren.

The time is now. We must move beyond rhetoric. We must move beyond recognition of problems to working together, to have the common efforts to build that common ground we hope to see.

God's blessing on you, your work, and all who will benefit from it. Godspeed and thank you very much.

[5] The weekend's V-J observances commemorated the fiftieth anniversary of Japan's World War II surrender. The United States and China both fought Japan during the war, but the Chinese population suffered huge military and civilian losses and large-scale atrocities, including mass rape, at the hands of the occupying Imperial Japanese Army from the mid-1930s on. Here, Hillary Clinton reminds her hosts that China and the United States fought together to defeat Imperial Japan.

> *At the press conference after our meeting... Yeltsin stole the show.... I almost fell over laughing. He could get away with saying the darnedest things.*
>
> —Bill Clinton, *My Life,* 2004

YELTSIN'S GIBE: After speaking at the United Nations, Russian President Boris Yeltsin traveled to President Franklin D. Roosevelt's historic home in Hyde Park, New York, for his ninth official summit meeting with Bill Clinton. Clinton enjoyed showing Yeltsin FDR's personal effects and letters, including a handwritten note to Stalin announcing the exact date of D-Day.

At the time, Clinton and Yeltsin needed each other: Yeltsin had to show Russians some tangible benefits of Western cooperation, and Clinton required Yeltsin's help to pacify the Bosnian Serbs in the run-up to the Dayton Peace Talks. After the meeting, the two world leaders held a press conference. Yeltsin told the gathered reporters and cameramen that, despite predictions in the press that the meeting would be a disaster, he was actually more optimistic after talking to Clinton. "Well, now, for the first time," Yeltsin announced to the American press, "I can tell you that you're a disaster!" At that, Clinton cracked up.

Photograph by Ralph Alswang

FUNERAL FOR A FRIEND: On November 4, 1995, a right-wing Israeli extremist assassinated Prime Minister Yitzhak Rabin during a peace rally in Tel Aviv. "I had come to love him as I had rarely loved another man," Clinton later wrote of Rabin, a liberal politician and co-recipient of the 1994 Nobel Peace Prize. The grieving First Couple, **left**, and a large American delegation, including House Speaker Newt Gingrich, flew to Israel for Rabin's funeral in the middle of a nasty budget showdown between the president and congressional Republicans.

Nine days after the funeral, Speaker Gingrich told an audience that he had hardened the Republican bargaining position—forcing Clinton's veto and shutting down the government—because of a perceived personal slight aboard Air Force One. The president, Gingrich said, wouldn't discuss the budget impasse with him during the trip. Worse yet, when Air Force One landed at Andrews Air Force Base, Clinton and former presidents Bush and Carter deplaned via the front door, while Gingrich and other congressional leaders were asked to use the rear exit.

"It's petty," said Gingrich, "but I think it's human. When you land at Andrews and you've been on the plane for twenty-five hours and nobody has talked to you and they ask you to get off by the back ramp…you just wonder, where is their sense of manners, where is their sense of courtesy?"

The next day, the *New York Daily News* ran a front-page cartoon depicting Gingrich as a crybaby throwing a tantrum. Then the White House released a photo, **above**, showing Gingrich, third from left, conversing with Clinton aboard Air Force One. The American public was left with the unmistakable impression that the speaker had shut down the US government in a fit of personal pique. The incident marked the beginning of Clinton's comeback from the disastrous 1994 midterm elections, and the beginning of the end for Gingrich's Republican revolution.

Photograph by Robert McNeely (facing page)

BOSNIAN INTERVENTION: One policy Clinton inherited from the Bush administration was a noninterventionist stance toward the ongoing conflict in Bosnia—a small multiethnic state created during the breakup of Yugoslavia. Orthodox Christian Serbs, who controlled neighboring Serbia, were outnumbered by Muslims and ethnic Croats inside Bosnia, but not outgunned. So the Serbs initiated a policy of "ethnic cleansing"—capturing, transporting, torturing, and killing Bosnian Muslims. The Serbian siege of the Bosnian capital of Sarajevo lasted nearly four years. And in July 1995, Serb forces massacred more than 8,000 Muslim men and boys in the eastern town of Srebrenica. After the Srebrenica massacre and a subsequent Serbian mortar attack on a Sarajevo marketplace, NATO warplanes—which had enforced a no-fly zone since 1993—began to actively hit Serb targets. That action helped US Secretary of State Warren Christopher bring the warring factions to Wright-Paterson Air Force Base outside Dayton, Ohio, for peace talks.

Talks began on November 1, 1995. Three weeks later, the parties emerged with the Dayton Accords—an agreement that carved Bosnia-Herzegovina into three autonomous regions, but preserved the state. Four days later, President Clinton, **above**, addressed the nation, seeking public support to send 20,000 US troops to help NATO enforce the agreement on the ground. "In the choice between peace and war," Clinton declared, "America must choose peace." Clinton had another longer-term motive. "Standing up for the Bosnians," he later wrote, "would demonstrate to Muslims the world over that the United States cared about them, respected Islam, and would support them if they rejected terror and embraced the possibilities of peace and reconciliation."

Photograph by Greg Gibson

PEACE TREATY: The Bosnian peace treaty was brokered in Dayton, Ohio, but signed the following month in Paris. International leaders applaud as, **above**, **l—r**, Serbian President Slobodan Milosevic, Croatian President Franjo Tudjman, and Bosnian President Alija Izetbegovic endorse the agreement at the Élysée Palace on December 14, 1995. The accords were also signed by, standing, **l—r**, Spanish Prime Minister Felipe Gonzalez, Clinton, French President Jacques Chirac, German Chancellor Helmut Kohl, British Prime Minister John Major, and Russian Prime Minister Viktor Chernomyrdin. Russian support was critical given the historic Slavic alliance between Russia and Serbia. At **left**, Clinton and Chirac chat during the signing ceremony.

Photograph by Peter Turnley (above)

PROTESTANTS: After brokering peace in the Balkans, Clinton traveled to Northern Ireland, where, on November 30, 1995, he met separately with Protestant firebrand Ian Paisley, **above**, and Catholic Sinn Fein leader Gerry Adams, **facing page**.

Beginning in January 1994, Clinton made good on a campaign promise to Irish American voters by turning his attention toward Northern Ireland's bloody "Troubles"—a religious conflict that had killed more than 3,000 people during the previous two decades. First, Clinton granted a US visa to Gerry Adams, leader of Sinn Fein, the political arm of the Irish Republican Army. That move upset the British government, which viewed Adams as a terrorist. A year later, Clinton appointed former Senate majority leader George Mitchell as the US special envoy for Northern Ireland. He devised the Mitchell Principles, a set of six conditions for peace talks that included, most importantly, disarming paramilitary groups on both sides. The resulting accord, the complex Belfast Agreement, was signed by all parties on April 10, 1998, and ratified by voters in both Northern Ireland and the Irish Republic a month later.

Photograph by Robert McNeely

CATHOLICS: Clinton speaks with Sinn Fein leader Gerry Adams during his visit to Belfast—the first trip to Northern Ireland by an American president. Clinton's success in reconciling militant Protestant unionists who wanted to maintain Northern Ireland's historic ties to Great Britain and a militant Catholic minority that wanted to reunite with the Republic of Ireland consolidated the American president's reputation as an international peacemaker.

Photograph by Robert McNeely

WHITE HOUSE CHRISTMAS: On December 3, 1995, in the Blue Room, Hillary Clinton helps trim the official White House Christmas tree—a Fraser fir from North Carolina. The first lady is joined by, **l–r**, famed mezzo-soprano Marilyn Horne, Academy Award winner Sidney Poitier, and blues legend B. B. King—all wearing their recently received Kennedy Center honoree medals.

Beginning with Jacqueline Kennedy in 1961, the first lady has traditionally chosen the annual theme for the White House Christmas tree. For the 1995 edition, Hillary asked architectural students nationwide to submit original ornaments inspired by Clement Clarke Moore's classic poem "A Visit from St. Nicholas" (better known by its first line, "'Twas the night before Christmas"). The resulting blizzard of baubles, **right**, mesmerizes the president.

Photographs by Robert McNeely

THEIR STORY IN PHOTOGRAPHS **161**

GUT REACTION: Between two government shutdowns, Speaker of the House Newt Gingrich and President Clinton share a laugh during a casual, post-meeting moment in the Cabinet Room. In the run-up to the 1994 midterm elections, Gingrich had branded Clinton "the enemy of normal Americans" and characterized the president and first lady as "counterculture McGovernicks." Clinton, on the other hand, was intrigued by Gingrich and impressed by his political skills. After the shellacking Democrats took in the midterms, Clinton said he looked forward to the opportunity to "compare our New Democratic ideas on economic and social problems with those embodied in the 'Contract with America.'" "Politics at its best," he wrote, "is about the competition of ideas and policy."

Photograph by Robert McNeely

OVAL OFFICE SCENES: Hillary tells Bill a secret, **top**, as White House Chief of Staff Leon Panetta checks his notes. Panetta—a talented Washington insider—replaced Bill's childhood friend Mack McLarty in the chief of staff role. The former congressman and OMB director (and future CIA director and secretary of state under Barack Obama) made the Clinton White House run far more efficiently.

Clinton, **bottom**, headed into the 1996 election year with an optimistic outlook. His recent accomplishments: nursing the economy back from recession, cutting the deficit, rescuing Mexico from financial disaster, soothing the nation after the Oklahoma City bombing, and facilitating peace in the Middle East, the Balkans, and Northern Ireland.

Photographs by Robert McNeely

Until you've testified at least five times before a grand jury like I have, you're just small potatoes.

—An unnamed White House aide to Hillary Clinton, after she testified before the Whitewater grand jury, 1996

IT TAKES A GRAND JURY: Ten-year-old Daniella Fortuna introduces the first lady, **facing page, top left**, at a Beverly Hills benefit for Los Angeles Children's Hospital on February 7, 1996. Hillary was on a ten-city publicity tour for her newly published book, *It Takes a Village: And Other Lessons Children Teach Us.* The *New York Times* best seller mixed personal anecdotes with heartfelt prescriptions for child rearing. Predictably, conservative critics attacked the book as thinly veiled socialism. At the Republican National Convention later that year, candidate Bob Dole would say, "With all due respect, I am here to tell you, it does not take a village to raise a child. It takes a family to raise a child."

During her book tour, Hillary learned that independent counsel Kenneth Starr would subpoena her to testify before a grand jury investigating Madison Guaranty Savings and Loan—a failed Arkansas thrift run by her old Whitewater partner Jim McDougal. It was the first time in US history that a president's wife had been subpoenaed, and Hillary had reason to worry. When she was an attorney at Rose Law Firm, she had done legal work for Madison Guaranty. Her old billing records, subpoenaed by Starr, were lost and then found, by a White House staffer, exposing Hillary to an obstruction of justice indictment. After a four-hour session before the grand jury on January 26, 1996, Clinton, **facing page, right**, answered questions from reporters before climbing into her limo for the ride back to the White House, **facing page, bottom left**.

Photographs by Vince Bucci (facing page, top left), Mark Wilson (facing page, bottom left), and Denis Paquin (facing page, right)

Each of us played the part of our daughters in the Sidwell Friends School Mother-Daughter Show. My role involved a lot of pirouetting like a ballerina.

—Hillary Rodham Clinton, *Living History,* 2003

STYLE AND SUBSTANCE: On the White House putting green, the president hones his short game while sixteen-year-old Chelsea, a student at the Washington Ballet School, practices her jetés—something she did so often that Hillary lampooned Chelsea's ballet moves at the Sidwell Friends School Mother-Daughter Show.

During the tumultuous 1996 election year, Chelsea would announce her intention to go to Stanford University, and her father would rack up an unlikely series of legislative wins in the Republican-controlled Congress. First came Megan's Law, which authorized states to notify the public about convicted sex offenders living or working in their communities. Then Clinton raised the federal minimum wage for the first time in five years—from $4.25 to $4.75. Next, the president won approval for the Health Insurance Portability and Accountability Act—better known today by its acronym, HIPAA—which protected health insurance coverage for workers who changed or lost their jobs. Finally, the Welfare Reform Act of 1996 ended guaranteed cash payments to the poor, imposed time limits on payments, and required welfare recipients to work in order to receive support. By cooperating with the president to pass such an impressive raft of legislation in such a short period of time, the Republican Congress helped ensure its own reelection, but effectively torpedoed Clinton's presidential challenger, Republican Majority Leader Bob Dole.

Megan's Law, May 17, 1996   **Photograph by Denis Paquin**

Raising the minimum wage, August 20, 1996   **Photograph by Ruth Fremson**

Health Insurance Portability and Accountability Act **(HIPAA)**, August 21, 1996
Photograph by Ruth Fremson

Welfare Reform Act of 1996, August 22, 1996

BRIDGE TO THE TWENTY-FIRST CENTURY: On August 29, 1996, in Chicago's United Center, Bill Clinton, **left**, accepts the nomination of the Democratic Party to seek a second term as president of the United States. Two weeks earlier, the Republicans had settled on their challenger, seventy-three-year-old Kansas Senator Bob Dole. Accepting the nomination, Dole argued, "Age has its advantages. Let me be the bridge to an America that only the unknowing call myth. Let me be the bridge to a time of tranquility, faith, and confidence in action." In his own acceptance speech, Clinton answered with a bit of verbal jujitsu: "With all respect," he said, "we do not need to build a bridge to the past. We need to build a bridge to the future. And that is what I commit to you to do. So tonight, let us resolve to build that bridge to the twenty-first century, to meet our challenges and protect our values."

In South Dakota for the final election rally of the campaign, Clinton, **above**, pumps up the crowd with senior advisor Doug Sosnik and press secretary Mike McCurry by his side.

Photograph by Robert McNeely (above)

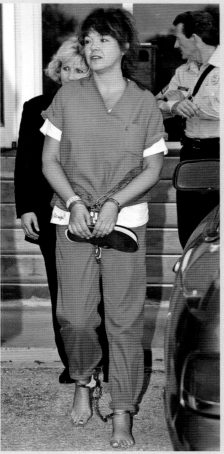

DEFENDERS: The president, **facing page**, tells the nation about the bomb and missile attacks he ordered against Iraqi forces on September 3, 1996. Clinton explained that the United States had made good on its guarantee to punish Saddam if he attacked ethnic Kurds within the UN-designated safe zone. Defense Secretary William Perry, **above**, explains that, in concert with the US action, the United Nations had extended its "no-fly zone" north to the thirty-third parallel.

More than two and a half years into the Whitewater investigation, collateral damage was still piling up. On September 13, 1996, Susan McDougal, the Clintons' partner in the failed Whitewater real estate deal, **left**, returns to jail for contempt of court after refusing to testify against the president before Kenneth Starr's grand jury. (McDougal was carrying her shoes because she said they hurt her feet.) "Whitewater wasn't about Whitewater anymore," Bill Clinton later wrote. "It was about whatever Ken Starr could dig up on anybody in Arkansas or my administration."

Photographs by Denis Paquin (facing page), Jamal Wilson (above), and Danny Johnston (left)

FOUR MORE YEARS: With the economy humming, the deficit declining, and the country, for the most part, at peace, the president easily trounced Republican Bob Dole and Texas businessman Ross Perot in the 1996 presidential contest. Clinton won thirty-one states and 49.2 percent of the ballots cast, becoming the first Democratic president to win reelection since Franklin D. Roosevelt a half century earlier. On election night, the Clinton family, **above**, returned to Little Rock for their second Old State House victory celebration. Then, on January 20, 1997, Chief Justice William Rehnquist, **facing page, top**, administered the oath of office. In her memoir, *Living History,* Hillary clearly remembered the moment after the swearing-in, when the conservative justice shook her husband's hand: "'Good luck,' Rehnquist said without smiling. Something about his tone made me think we would need it."

During the inaugural parade, **facing page**, **bottom**, the Clinton family walked the last few blocks to the White House. "I felt I was entering this new chapter in my life, like steel tempered in fire," Hillary later wrote, "a bit harder at the edges but more durable, more flexible."

FLYING HIGH: The day after the 1996 presidential election, Bill and Hillary, **facing page** and **top**, flew from Little Rock to Washington aboard Air Force One. Although Clinton won decisively, he had no coattails. The Democrats lost three Senate seats and gained only three House seats, so Congress remained firmly in Republican hands. Sobered by the wide-ranging Whitewater investigation and the collapse of her health care initiative, Hillary's role in the White House pivoted. In the second term, the first lady said, she hoped to shape White House policy on issues that affected women, children, and families.

"We don't have a moment to waste," Clinton, **bottom**, declared in his February 4, 1997, State of the Union address. "Tomorrow there will be just over one thousand days until the year 2000. One thousand days to prepare our people. One thousand days to work together. One thousand days to build a bridge to a land of new promise."

Photographs by Robert McNeely

BALANCING ACT: On August 5, 1996, the president, **above**, signed his first balanced budget. Clinton's tax hike three years earlier helped reduce the deficit every year during his first term. Then the booming 1990s economy, huge run-ups in the stock market, the dot-com bubble, and a Social Security surplus increased revenues to the point where the government took in more than it spent every fiscal year during Clinton's second term.

WELCOME TO THE CLUB, BORIS: In June 1997, **left, l–r**, Japanese Prime Minister Ryutaro Hashimoto, Canadian Prime Minister Jean Chrétien, British Prime Minister Tony Blair, Russian President Boris Yeltsin, Bill Clinton, French President Jacques Chirac, German Chancellor Helmut Kohl, and Italian Prime Minister Romano Prodi pose with Jacques Santer of the European Commission and Wim Kok of the European Council at the twenty-third annual G7 economic summit, held in Denver, Colorado. That year, the G7— short for the "Group of Seven" industrialized nations—admitted Russia and became the G8. Russia's inclusion in the exclusive club came at Bill Clinton's urging, and as Clinton hoped, the resulting prestige helped Boris Yeltsin shore up his precarious political position at home.

PRESIDENTIAL COMPANIONS: Bill and Hillary, **above**, attend a meeting in the Oval Office. Also in the Oval Office, **facing page, top**: Buddy the chocolate Labrador retriever, still a puppy. The president acquired Buddy in late 1997 and named him after his late great-uncle, Henry "Buddy" Grisham. Buddy's mortal enemy was Socks the cat. At Camp David, **facing page, bottom**, Clinton helps his new secretary of state, Madeleine Albright, hone her bowling skills at the presidential retreat's two-lane alley.

Photograph by Robert McNeely (above)

"I did not have sexual relations with that woman, Miss Lewinsky. I never told any-body to lie, not a single time. Never. These allegations are false." —Bill Clinton

"No matter who the man is, nobody can treat you like this and use you and just throw you out the door like some piece of meat."—Paula Corbin Jones

MONICA, PAULA, AND KEN, OH MY!: In early 1998, two sex scandals rocked the Clinton presidency. On January 21, the *Washington Post* reported that prosecutor Kenneth Starr had expanded his Whitewater probe to include alleged efforts to convince former White House intern Monica Lewinsky to lie under oath about a sexual affair with the president. The Lewinsky story—first reported on the Internet by Matt Drudge, then pounced upon by every news organization in the country—riveted the nation, and on January 26, the independent counsel, **above**, met the media horde.

Later that day—at a White House press conference touting federal child care programs—the president, **facing page**, **top**, confronted the Lewinsky firestorm head on. With Hillary and Al Gore standing behind him, Clinton wagged his finger and famously announced, "I did not have sexual relations with that woman, Miss Lewinsky." Clinton's emphatic statement was, by nearly every measure, untrue. And he similarly dissembled under oath during a separate, long-running sexual harassment lawsuit brought by former Arkansas state employee Paula Jones, **facing page**, **bottom**. The Jones case, the first civil lawsuit against a sitting president ever allowed to go forward, was managed and funded by what Hillary Clinton would soon dub "a vast right-wing conspiracy." In the end, Clinton would settle the Jones case with an $850,000 payment, but he would never apologize or admit guilt. The Republicans, meanwhile, would use the president's testimony in *Jones v. Clinton* as a basis for impeachment.

On January 27, 1998, the day after he denied his affair with Monica Lewinsky, the president delivered his State of the Union address, reporting the creation of 14 million new jobs and the reduction of the federal government to its smallest size in thirty-five years. But that bit of historic news was largely lost in the media uproar over the president's alleged sexual misconduct.

Photographs by Diana Walker (facing page, top) and Richard Ellis (above)

FOREIGN RELATIONS: In March 1998, Bill Clinton visited the southern tip of Africa, where President Nelson Mandela, **facing page, top**, showed him the view from his old Robben Island jail cell. Mandela spent eighteen of his twenty-seven years as a political prisoner on the cold, windswept island.

On May 18, 1998, the day after a G8 summit in Birmingham, England, the president—beleaguered at home by the Lewinsky scandal—dropped by 10 Downing Street to visit his ideological protégé, Prime Minister Tony Blair, **facing page**, **bottom**. A few days earlier, Clinton lent moral support to German Chancellor Helmut Kohl at the thousand-year-old Wartburg Castle in Eisenach, **above**. Kohl, the longest-serving German chancellor in more than a century, had presided over the reunification of Germany, but he would be defeated in October 1998 by Social Democrat Gerhard Schröder.

Photograph by J. Scott Applewhite (facing page, top)

FETCH: Bill and Buddy on the White House lawn, July 11, 1998.

TERROR STRIKES AGAIN: On August 7, 1998, massive truck bombs simultaneously destroyed two US embassies in East Africa. In central Nairobi, Kenya, 212 people were killed and approximately 4,000 wounded. In Dar es Salaam, Tanzania, where the US Embassy was on the outskirts of town, 11 died and 85 were wounded. The attacks—which coincided with the eighth anniversary of American troops arriving in Saudi Arabia for the first Gulf War—were perpetrated by Egyptian Islamic Jihad in concert with an ambitious forty-one-year-old Saudi terrorist named Osama bin Laden.

The day after the bombings, the president, **facing page**, addressed the nation from the Oval Office. He promised, "No matter how long it takes or where it takes us, we will pursue terrorists until the cases are solved and justice is done." In Osama bin Laden's case, it would take two more major assaults—the October 2000 USS Cole bombing and the massive 9/11/2001 attacks—and nearly thirteen years to bring him to justice. (Clinton's quick retaliation on suspected al-Qaeda sites in Afghanistan and Somalia was criticized as a "wag the dog" diversion by GOP lawmakers focused on Clinton's impeachment.)

On August 13, 1998, the emotional president and first lady, **above**, view coffins carrying the remains of ten Americans killed in the blast. At **left**, a US Marine consults with an FBI investigator in front of the bombed US Embassy in Dar es Salaam.

Photographs by Joe Marquette (above), Brennan Linsley (left), and Ruth Fremson (facing page)

'FESSING UP: After answering Whitewater prosecutors' pointed questions about his Lewinsky affair for four hours—a session independent counsel Kenneth Starr videotaped for future use—the president prepares to speak to the nation on August 17, 1998. Still fuming about the lascivious and humiliating nature of the cross-examination—"pornographic," in Clinton's words—the president desperately wanted to lash out at Starr, but in the end he managed to control his famous temper. In his televised statement, Clinton admitted that his relationship with Lewinsky was "not appropriate" and that he had "misled people, including even my wife." Then he said that the investigation "had gone on too long, cost too much and hurt too many people.... It is time," he said, "to stop the pursuit of personal destruction and get on with our national life." Clinton hoped that his televised mea culpa would derail the impeachment effort gathering steam in Congress, but independent counsel Ken Starr and Speaker Newt Gingrich's House Republicans were determined to move forward.

Photograph by Greg Gibson

STARR WITNESS: On August 20, 1998, former White House intern Monica Lewinsky arrives at the federal courthouse in Washington, DC, for her second day of testimony in front of Kenneth Starr's grand jury. Lewinsky's answers were far more graphic than the president's. She revealed intimate details about her sexual encounters with Clinton, but denied any allegation that the White House had instructed her to lie or offered her a job to buy her silence. The next month, the independent counsel presented the 453-page *Starr Report* to the House Judiciary Committee. The Republican-controlled committee quickly posted the sexually explicit report on the Internet—along with more than 3,000 pages of graphic evidence designed to humiliate the president. In response, more than seventy US newspapers called on Clinton to resign.

SCENES FROM AN IMPEACHMENT: On December 19, 1998, the president and first lady, **above**, meet reporters outside the Oval Office. The Republican-controlled House of Representatives had just voted to impeach the president on two counts: perjury before Ken Starr's grand jury and obstruction of justice in the Paula Jones sexual harassment suit. Two other articles of impeachment—perjury in the Jones case and making perjurious statements to Congress—failed. Al and Tipper Gore and a phalanx of Democratic legislators stood by Clinton at the press event. The vice president made a heartfelt statement calling the impeachment "a great disservice to a man I believe will be regarded in the history books as one of our greatest presidents." During the three-month impeachment process, Al Gore and Hillary Clinton's approval ratings would soar. Perhaps more surprisingly, the president's approval rating would rise to nearly 70 percent—the highest of his presidency—and remain there until the end of his term. At **left**, a monitor on Capitol Hill shows the videotape of Clinton's grand jury testimony—including Clinton's famous parsing of the word "is"—as it is fed to television networks.

Photographs by Tim Sloan (above) and Ken Lambert (left)

PROSECUTORIAL ZEAL: Speaker of the House Newt Gingrich, **above**, makes his way through a crowd of cameras after the House of Representatives authorized the judiciary committee to conduct an impeachment inquiry against the president on October 8, 1998. A month later, after disappointing midterm elections, Gingrich surprised the nation by announcing that he would step down from the speakership and resign his House seat after ten full terms. As *Time* magazine noted, "Clinton has an affair with an intern, and Gingrich loses his job over it." At **right**, independent counsel Ken Starr is sworn in before the House Judiciary Committee impeachment inquiry on November 19, 1998. Starr testified that President Clinton had misused "the machinery of government" to illegally interfere with the Paula Jones sexual harassment lawsuit and the Monica Lewinsky investigation. Neither charge would stick in the Senate, but Clinton would eventually pay a $90,000 contempt of court fine and agree to a five-year suspension of his Arkansas law license.

Photographs by Justin Lane (above) and Luke Frazza (right)

MOVING ON: In the midst of an impeachment trial most Americans didn't want to see, President Clinton, **left**, gave his seventh State of the Union address. The president's eighty-minute speech touted the largest federal budget surplus—and what would soon be the longest economic expansion—in American history. Looking ahead, Clinton talked about a minimum wage increase, using the budget surplus to ensure Social Security's long-term viability, tougher standards for teachers, investing in schools, and protecting the nation's computer networks. He never mentioned the elephant in the room: his own impeachment. (Nor did he mention the de facto repeal of the Depression-era Glass-Steagall Act that he would sign ten months later—a change that allowed commercial banks to get into the investment business and would later contribute to the 2008 world financial meltdown.)

Demonstrators supporting President Clinton, **above**, took to the streets in Los Angeles on December 16, 1998. Disgust with the relentlessly partisan campaign to remove the popular president from office among younger, tech-savvy voters spawned MoveOn.org, an early example of online activism. MoveOn collected 500,000 "electronic signatures" from Americans who called on Congress to censure the president—and move on. On February 12, 1999, after a stirring closing argument by former Arkansas senator Dale Bumpers, the Senate, which had fifty-five Republican members at the time, voted not to convict on either count—55–45 against the perjury charge and a 50–50 tie on the obstruction of justice charge. Both tallies fell well short of the two-thirds majority required for conviction.

Photograph by Dan Callister (above)

KOSOVO FORCE: On April 22, 1999, Bill Clinton addresses NATO "Kosovo Force" troops in the Macedonian capital of Skopje. They were there to assist hundreds of thousands of Muslim refugees who were flooding into Macedonia from the neighboring Serbian province of Kosovo. Three years after the Dayton Accords ended the bloody conflict in Bosnia, Slobodan Milosevic's Serbian forces were attacking Kosovo's Muslim majority, who had declared Kosovo an independent state.

A ten-week NATO bombing campaign against Serbian military targets and a threat to deploy NATO ground forces finally forced Milosevic to withdraw his troops from Kosovo, but not before 11,000 people died and 1.3 million Muslims were displaced. Throughout the crisis, some criticized Clinton's hesitance to use ground forces to stop the killing; others questioned the legality of the entire operation; and some Republicans continued to question the president's qualifications as commander in chief. "Our strategy would often be second-guessed," Clinton later wrote, "but never abandoned."

Photograph by Cynthia Johnson (facing page)

KOSOVAR REFUGEES: On May 14, 1999, Hillary Clinton visits Stenkovec Refugee Camp in Macedonia, temporary home to 20,000 Kosovar refugees. At the time, Democratic Party leaders were pressing Hillary to run for the Senate seat vacated by retiring New York senator Daniel Patrick Moynihan. Hillary weighed the pros and cons as she traveled the world on behalf of the big issues that had always motivated her: human rights, women's rights, universal access to medical care, religious tolerance, and the plight of refugees.

Photograph by Tyler Hicks (above)

RUNNING: Armed with sky-high approval ratings, a wardrobe that included six black pantsuits, and a plan to visit every one of New York state's sixty-two counties, the first lady of the United States formally announces her candidacy for the US Senate in Purchase, New York, on February 6, 2000, **facing page**. Backing her, **l–r**, are Congressman Charlie Rangel of New York, state Democratic Party chair Judith Hope, New York Senator Charles Schumer, retiring senator Daniel Patrick Moynihan, President Bill Clinton, Chelsea Clinton; and Hillary's mother, Dorothy Rodham. With that, Hillary became the first and only presidential spouse ever to run for national office. In March, CBS news anchor Dan Rather asked Clinton if he expected to be the husband of a US senator. He answered that he had no idea, but if Hillary won, "she would be magnificent."

MARCHING: "I loved that day in Selma," Clinton wrote in his memoir, *My Life*. "Once again, I was swept back across the years to my boyhood longing for, and belief in, an America without a racial divide." Clinton was referring to a bright Sunday in March 2000, when civil rights leaders gathered in Selma, Alabama, to commemorate the thirty-fifth anniversary of the watershed confrontation between police and voting-rights marchers on Selma's Edmund Pettus Bridge. Arm in arm with Clinton are the Reverend Jesse Jackson, Coretta Scott King, and Georgia congressman and civil rights icon John Lewis.

LAST-CHANCE SUMMITRY: Bill Clinton was determined to leave office with a lasting Israeli-Palestinian peace accord that would help to stabilize the entire Middle Eastern region. For two weeks, high-level Israeli and Palestinian diplomats negotiated in the seclusion of Camp David under the supervision of Israeli Prime Minister Ehud Barak and PLO Chairman Yasir Arafat. But it was not to be. In the closing days of Clinton's term, Arafat walked away from a deal shaped by the president and backed by the Israelis, over apparently minor issues. To Clinton, it was an blunder of historic proportions—and one of the biggest foreign policy disappointments of his presidency.

SECOND CHANCES: The First Couple shares a tender kiss just after senatorial candidate Hillary Clinton introduces her husband at the Hollywood Gala Salute to President William Jefferson Clinton, held at a Brentwood estate on August 12, 2000. The star-studded gala celebrating Clinton's presidency was also a fund-raiser for Hillary's Senate campaign. As it turned out, the event broke campaign finance laws, and some of the organizers were subsequently convicted of unrelated felonies—but that night Hollywood's stars came out to honor the Clintons and enjoy performances by Diana Ross, Cher, Toni Braxton, Patti LaBelle, Sugar Ray, and Michael Bolton. Bill, who spent months in Hillary's doghouse after he was forced to reveal his affair with Monica Lewinsky, lent enthusiastic support to his wife's campaign.

Photograph by Khue Bui

SENATOR CLINTON: On November 7, 2000, First Lady Hillary Rodham Clinton—joined by her husband, her daughter, and a crowd of thousands at New York's Grand Hyatt Hotel—savors her decisive 55 to 43 percent victory over Republican Rick Lazio. Hillary's original opponent, popular New York mayor Rudy Giuliani, dropped out of the race in the spring after he was diagnosed with prostate cancer, separated from his wife, and took up with another woman. Giuliani's replacement, a young Long Island congressman, won most of New York's upstate counties but fell well short in New York City and its northern suburbs.

That night Hillary became the first woman elected to the US Senate from New York and the only American first lady to ever win public office. In her memoir, *Living History,* Hillary wrote, "The tables were now turned, as [Bill] now played for me the role I had always played for him. Once he had given his advice, it was my decision to make."

Photographs by Stephen Jaffe (above) and Susan Watts (right)

FROM CHAPPAQUA TO HANOI: Stanford University senior Chelsea Clinton and her dad, **facing page**, talk things over in their family's new home in suburban Chappaqua, New York. The Clintons bought the $1.7 million five-bedroom, four-bath Dutch Colonial—their first private residence in nearly two decades—so that Hillary could establish New York residency for her Senate run. Denizens of the upper-middle-class—but hardly posh—commuter town were surprised to learn that the sitting president of the United States had moved in down the street. Until then, Chappaqua's only celebrity was singer Vanessa Williams.

Ten days later, the president brought Chelsea to Hanoi, **above**, where he pressed the flesh, American style. Clinton—who had protested the Vietnam War while he was a Rhodes Scholar at Oxford and managed to avoid the draft through deft use of his political connections—was the first US president to visit the country in thirty years. He told the Vietnamese people, "We wish to be your partners."

THE PRESIDENT AND THE SENATOR: On January 3, 2001, US Vice President and President of the Senate Al Gore, **above**, swears in the freshman senator from New York, as Bill and Chelsea hold the Bible. Bill's presidential term and Hillary's term as senator overlapped by seventeen days—the only time in US history that a married couple served in the White House and Senate simultaneously. Three weeks earlier, Gore's own quest for the presidency was cut short when the Supreme Court stopped a recount in closely contested Florida, effectively calling the election for Republican George W. Bush. As a result, Gore, who won the popular vote by more than half a million ballots, lost in the electoral college by five votes—the closest electoral tally since 1876. On the **facing page**, the president and first lady enjoy a quiet moment during their last days in the White House.

CHANGING OF THE GUARD: Bill Clinton and his successor, George W. Bush, **above**, meet at the White House on December 19, 2000. In his memoir, Clinton remembered that the two men talked about security issues, with Clinton stressing the dangers of known terrorist Osama bin Laden and his al-Qaeda network.

The last morning of Bill Clinton's presidency, January 20, 2001, was cold and rainy. President Clinton, **left**, spent a quiet moment in the Oval Office waiting for President-elect George W. Bush and his wife, Laura, to stop by for coffee and pastries before the Clintons and Bushes drove to the Capitol together for Bush's Inauguration. On the Resolute desk is the letter that the sitting president traditionally leaves for his successor. Eight years earlier, Clinton received a similar letter from Bush's father.

HERS: Published in June 2003, Hillary Clinton's autobiography, *Living History,* earned its author a breathtaking $8 million advance from publisher Simon & Schuster—second only to the record advance reportedly paid to Pope John Paul II for his memoir. Defying skeptics, Hillary's tale sold more than a million copies in its first year. **Above**: On the day of its release, June 9, 2003, Hillary appears at a Barnes & Noble bookstore in New York to sign copies.

Photograph by Chris Hondros

HIS: On June 23, 2004, Bill Clinton fans line up at the downtown Borders Books in New York City to get signed copies of the former president's 957–page memoir, *My Life*. Four years after he left office, Clinton's approval rating was high and rising as Americans looked back wistfully at the booming 1990s. The nostalgia paid off: between *My Life* and his 2007 tract, *Giving: How Each of Us Can Change the World*, Clinton earned a reported $30 million.

Photograph by Debra L. Rothenberg

WORKHORSE: Three years into her first Senate term, Hillary Clinton joined the Armed Services Committee, a rare and powerful post for a freshman senator. By all accounts, she earned it. Colleagues and pundits alike began to call her a "workhorse" as she avoided the media glare, built a first-class staff, and mastered complex policy issues. Senator Clinton is photographed, **above**, at a Washington, DC, hotel and, **facing page, top**, in the President's Room, just off the Senate floor, both in May 2006.

In August 2008, Clinton, **facing page**, **bottom**, listens as Secretary of Defense Donald Rumsfeld, General John Abizaid, and General Peter Pace, chairman of the Joint Chiefs of Staff, testify about the ongoing Iraq war during a Senate Armed Services Committee hearing. "You are presiding over a failed policy," Clinton told Rumsfeld at the hearing. Later that year, Clinton would be reelected with 67 percent of the vote, winning all but four of New York's sixty-two counties.

Photographs by Diana Walker (above and facing page, top) and Mark Wilson (facing page, bottom)

MRS. CLINTON

Be a workhorse, not a show horse. Accept being at the bottom of the totem pole, and go from there.

—Veteran senator Robert Byrd's advice to freshman senator Hillary Rodham Clinton

THE TOP JOB: On January 20, 2007—four days after a little-known freshman senator named Barack Obama announced he was exploring a White House run—Hillary answered with her own presidential exploratory committee. "I'm in. And I'm in to win," she said in her webcast. With that, the well-known, well-funded, and well-connected New York senator immediately became the Democratic front-runner and the first woman with a real shot at the White House.

Chelsea Clinton, **above**, carries her mother's message to young voters at the University of Delaware on February 4, 2008. At **left**, buttons on sale at a Davenport rally in advance of Iowa's Democratic Party caucuses. On the **facing page**, two days before the Iowa caucuses, Hillary Clinton speaks at the Sioux City Art Center. Despite a steady lead among Democratic candidates in early national polling, Clinton finished behind Senator Obama and Senator John Edwards of North Carolina in the first contest of the Democratic primary season—an outcome that hinted at problems to come.

Photographs by Scott Olson (left) and Michael Appleton (facing page)

EIGHTEEN MILLION CRACKS: Democratic presidential hopeful Hillary Clinton, **left**, speaks to a sea of supporters at her campaign's Super Tuesday rally in New York on February 5, 2008. Twenty-three states and territories held Democratic primaries or caucuses that day, and in the end, Barack Obama emerged with slightly more delegates than Hillary. **Above**, Chelsea and former President Bill Clinton stand front and center as Hillary addresses an enthusiastic crowd at the University of Pennsylvania on the day before the April 5, 2008, Pennsylvania primary. Hillary beat Obama decisively in the Keystone State, but by that point she was playing catch-up.

The bruising primary season would drag on until June 7, when Clinton gracefully conceded. In her concession speech, the woman who came the closest in history to winning a major-party presidential nomination in the United States with more than 18 million votes, said, "Although we weren't able to shatter that highest, hardest glass ceiling this time, thanks to you, it's got about 18 million cracks in it. And the light is shining through like never before, filling us all with the hope and the sure knowledge that the path will be a little easier next time."

Among pundits there was much debate as to why Hillary had failed to galvanize the Democratic Party. Many pointed to her 2003 Senate vote giving President Bush the power to invade Iraq, which sharply contrasted with Senator Obama's steadfast opposition to the war from the get-go. "Her handling of the war issue subjected her to the kind of broader examination she wasn't expecting," said a former Democratic senator and supporter. "It put her in a position of looking backward, not forward, of caving to conventional wisdom instead of moving in the direction of new leadership, new ideas, being bold." Senator Obama went on to win the Democratic nomination and decisively beat Republican John McCain in the general election.

Photographs by Chris Hondros (left) and Joe Raedle (above)

MADAME SECRETARY: In the Oval Office on the day after his inauguration, President Barack Obama, **above**, confers with his former opponent and new secretary of state, Hillary Rodham Clinton. "I have known Hillary Clinton as a friend, a colleague, a source of counsel, and as a campaign opponent," said President-elect Barack Obama when he announced Clinton as his pick for State. "She possesses an extraordinary intelligence and toughness, and a remarkable work ethic. Hillary's appointment is a sign to friend and foe of the seriousness of my commitment to renew American diplomacy and restore our alliances."

Hillary was quickly confirmed by the Senate and sworn in on January 21, 2009, the day after Obama's inauguration. In the years following, her steady hand at the State Department was highly praised and her approval ratings remained higher than ever before in her career. **Facing page**, **top**: Secretary Clinton and Afghani President Hamid Karzai leave a press conference at the State Department in Washington, DC, on May 11, 2010. **Facing page**, **bottom**: Two weeks later, Clinton addresses the media after a North Korean submarine torpedoed and sank a South Korean warship, killing forty-six.

Photographs by Pete Souza (above), Alex Wong (facing page, top), and Kim Min-Hee (facing page, bottom)

A NEW CHAPTER: Former President Bill Clinton, sixty-three, walks his daughter down the aisle. Chelsea, thirty, wed investment banker Marc Mezvinsky, thirty-two, in Rhinebeck, New York, on July 31, 2010. Veiled in secrecy, the wedding was dubbed the social event of the summer season, with more than 400 guests in attendance. A Jewish rabbi and a Methodist minister conducted the interfaith service, Chelsea's gown was by Vera Wang, and the setting was John Jacob Astor IV's 1902 estate overlooking the Hudson River.

The newlyweds took up residence in Manhattan. Also in Manhattan—farther north in Harlem—were the offices of the William J. Clinton Foundation, which initially supported emerging entrepreneurs, but evolved over time to address global issues such as poverty, climate change, and unequal access to health care and economic opportunity. In 2005, the former president founded the Clinton Global Initiative to inspire, connect, and empower a community of global leaders to alleviate poverty, create a cleaner environment, and increase access to health care and education. All in all, a productive post-presidency.

Photographs by Genevieve de Manio (left) and Barbara Kinney (above)

REFERENCES

Quotations used in this book are from the sources listed below:

7 Bill Clinton, *My Life,* Vintage Books, 2005.

8 Michael Takiff, *A Complicated Man: The Life of Bill Clinton by Those Who Know Him*, Yale University Press, 2010.

10 Clinton, *My Life.*

12 Ibid.

13 John Fairhall, "Clinton Opens Painful Childhood to Voters in Confessional Film Biography," *Baltimore Sun*, July 17, 1992; Hillary Clinton, *Living History*, Scribner, 2003.

15 Clinton, *Living History.*

16 Ibid.

18 Clinton, *My Life.*

21 Ibid.

23 "Bill Clinton's Draft Letter," *Frontline*, www.pbs.org/wgbh.

25 John Heilemann, "When They Were Young," *New York Magazine*, October 14, 2007.

26 Clinton, *Living History.*

26 Ibid.; Clinton, *My Life.*

27 Carl Bernstein, *A Woman in Charge: The Life of Hillary Rodham Clinton,* Vintage Books, 2007.

28 Clinton, *Living History.*

33 Ibid.

35 Clinton, *My Life.*

38 Bernstein, *A Woman in Charge.*

40 Clinton, *Living History.*

42 Takiff, *A Complicated Man.*

44 Todd S. Purdum, "Virginia Clinton, 70, President's Mother, Is Dead," *New York Times*, January 7, 1994.

46 Clinton, *My Life.*

50 Richard Poplak, "Chelsea Clinton Takes to the Airwaves," *Daily Maverick*, January 25, 2012.

54 "Clinton Bores His Audience, Crowd Cheers When Clinton Finishes His Speech," www.msnbc.msn.com.

55 Clinton, *Living History.*

56 Sidney Blumenthal, *The Clinton Wars*, Farrar, Straus and Giroux, 2003.

58 "Bill Clinton, Announcement Speech, Old State House, Little Rock, Arkansas, October 3, 1991," www.4president.org.

61 "Democratic Candidates Debate," www.c-spanvideo.org, December 15, 1991.

62 Bernstein, *A Woman in Charge.*

64 David Brock, *The Seduction of Hillary Rodham*, Simon & Schuster, 1998.

67 "In Their Own Words: Excerpts from Addresses by Keynote Speakers at Democratic Convention," *New York Times*, July 14, 1992; Clinton, *My Life.*

70 Clinton, *My Life.*

75–79 "First Inaugural Address (January 20, 1993)," www.millercenter.org/president/Clinton.

80 Clinton, *Living History.*

83 Takiff, *A Complicated Man;* Clinton, *My Life.*

85 Bernstein, *A Woman in Charge.*

86 Ibid.; Clinton, *Living History.*

89 "1993 State of the Union Address," www.washingtonpost.com, February 17, 1993.

90 Clinton, *Living History.*

92 Ibid.; Clinton, *My Life.*

94 John M. Broder, "Clinton, Nixon Join on Yeltsin Wavelength," *Los Angeles Times,* March 10, 1993.

95 Clinton, *Living History.*

96 "Interview: David Gergen," *Frontline*, www.pbs.org/wgbh, June 2000.

98 "Clinton Thanks Students for Opening White House Mail," Associated Press, June 13, 1998.

100 David Von Drehle and R. Jeffrey Smith, "U.S. Strikes Iraq for Plot to Kill Bush," *Washington Post*, June 27, 1993.

103 Clinton, *My Life.*

105 David E. Rosenbaum, "The Budget Struggle; Clinton Wins Approval of His Budget Plan as Gore Votes to Break Senate Deadlock," *New York Times*, August 7, 1993.

106 Clinton, *My Life.*

109 Ibid.

113 "Remarks on the Signing of NAFTA (December 8, 1993)," www.millercenter.org.

115 Clinton, *My Life.*

117 Jodi Enda, "A Stellar Debut Before Congress: Hillary Clinton Impresses with Charm and Political Savvy," *Philadelphia Inquirer*, September 29, 1993.

121 James E. Mueller, *Tag Teaming the Press: How Bill and Hillary Clinton Work Together to Handle the Media*, Rowman & Littlefield, 2008.

123 Rupert Cornwell, "Gore Trounces Perot in NAFTA Debate: Vice-President's Triumphant TV Performance Boosts White House Hopes," *Independent*, November 11, 1993.

125 Clinton, *My Life.*

126 Ibid.

130 Clinton, *Living History.*

132 George Stephanopoulos, *All Too Human: A Political Education*, Back Bay Books, 2000.

135 Clinton, *My Life.*

136 Ibid.

139–141 "1995 Oklahoma City Bombing Memorial Prayer Service Address," www.americanrhetoric.com.

144 *Wordplay,* directed by Patrick Creadon, 2006.

145 Bernstein, *A Woman in Charge.*

146–151 "Remarks to the Plenary Session of the United Nations Fourth World Conference on Women (1995)," www.americanrhetoric.com.

152 Clinton, *My Life.*

155 Ibid.; Alexander Nazaryan, "Newt Gingrich, Crybaby: The Famous Daily News Cover Explained," *New York Daily News*, January 6, 2012.

156 Clinton, *My Life.*

162 Ibid.

164 "Bob Dole's Acceptance Speech, August 15, 1996," www.pbs.org/newshour.

165 Clinton, *Living History.*

167 Ibid.

171 Thomas Hardy and Charles M. Madigan, "Dole to America: You Can Trust Me," *Chicago Tribune,* August 16, 1996; *Public Papers of the Presidents of the United States, William J. Clinton, Book I,* Office of the Federal Register, 1998.

173 Clinton, *My Life.*

174 Clinton, *Living History.*

177 "1997 State of the Union Address," *Washington Post,* February 4, 1997.

182 "Response to the Lewinsky Allegations (January 26, 1998) Bill Clinton," www.millercenter.org; "I Feel That I Have Won, Says Paula Jones," Associated Press, November 15, 1998.

188 *Public Papers of the Presidents of the United States, William J. Clinton, Book I.*

190 "President Bill Clinton (Transcript of Remarks)," www.cnn.com, August 17, 1998.

192 "The Impeachment Trial: President Clinton Responds," www.pbs.org/newshour.

193 Nancy Gibbs and Michael Duffy, "Fall of the House of Newt," *Time,* November 16, 1998.

197 Clinton, *My Life.*

199 Ibid.

202 Clinton, *Living History.*

205 Clay Chandler, "Clinton Urges Vietnam to Open Its Markets; In Ho Chi Minh City, President Extols Foreign Investment," **Washington Post,** November 20, 2000.

212 "Pentagon brass: Iraq civil war is possible," www.msnbc.msn.com, August 3, 2006.

213 Senator Jean Carnahan, "Byrd: The Greatest Roman of Them All," www.firedupmissouri.com, June 28, 2010.

214 "Clinton: 'I'm In, and I'm In to Win," Associated Press, January 21, 2007.

217 Debbie Walsh and Kathy Kleeman, "For a Woman to Reach the White House, the 2012 Elections Will Be Key," www.washingtonpost.com, April 1, 2011; Bernstein, *A Woman in Charge.*

218 Don Gonyea, "National Security Team Tasked with Obama's Vision," www.npr.org, December 2, 2008.

Note: Facts and figures about Clinton's budget surplus throughout this book are from www.factcheck.org (a project of the Annenberg Public Policy Center) and based on Congressional Budget Office data. (See www.factcheck.org/2008/02/the-budget-and-deficit-under-clinton/.) Note that Clinton's budgets include fiscal years 1994–2001.

The following books are among those used as sources:

Bernstein, Carl. *A Woman in Charge: The Life of Hillary Rodham Clinton.* New York: Vintage Books, 2007.

Blumenthal, Sidney. *The Clinton Wars.* New York: Farrar, Straus and Giroux, 2003.

Brock, David. *The Seduction of Hillary Rodham.* New York: Simon & Schuster, 1998.

Clinton, Bill. *My Life,* New York: Vintage Books. 2005.

Clinton, Hillary. *Living History.* New York: Scribner, 2003.

Hamilton, Nigel. *American Caesars: Lives of the Presidents from Franklin D. Roosevelt to George W. Bush.* New Haven: Yale University Press, 2010.

Maraniss, David. *The Clinton Enigma: A Four-and-a-Half Minute Speech Reveals This President's Entire Life.* New York: Simon & Schuster, 1998.

Mueller, James E. *Tag Teaming the Press: How Bill and Hillary Clinton Work Together to Handle the Media.* New York: Rowman & Littlefield, 2008.

Stephanopoulos, George. *All Too Human: A Political Education.* New York: Back Bay Books, 2000.

Takiff, Michael. *A Complicated Man: The Life of Bill Clinton by Those Who Know Him.* New Haven: Yale University Press, 2010.

The following websites are among those used as sources:

articles.latimes.com
www.baseball-almanac.com
www.bls.gov
   (Bureau of Labor Statistics)
www.bostonherald.com
www.brandeis.edu
www.cbsnews.com
www.clintonhousemuseum.org
www.clintonlibrary.gov
www.c-spanvideo.org
www.dol.gov
   (US Department of Labor)
www.encyclopediaofarkansas.net
www.factcheck.org
govinfo.library.unt.edu (University of North Texas)
www.haaretz.com
www.hillaryclintonquarterly.com
www.history.army.mil
www.history.org
www.history.navy.mil
www.historyplace.com
www.hotsprings.org
www.joshuaredman.com
www.lawcrossing.com
maboysstate.org
www.millercenter.org
   (University of Virginia)
www.nara.gov (National Archives and Records Administration)
www.nationalservice.gov
www.ncbi.nlm.nih.gov
   (National Center for Biotechnology Information)
news.bbc.co.uk
www.npr.org
www.nytimes.com
www.observer.com
www.pbs.org
www.people.com
www.saxophone-players-guide.com
www.sothebys.com
www.time.com
www.timeline-help.com
www.un.org
usconservatives.about.com
www.usconstitution.net
www.washingtonpost.com
www.wellesley.edu
www.wikipedia.org

PHOTOGRAPHY SOURCES

AFP/Getty: 73, 164, 173 (top), 192 (top), 193 (bottom), 202

Associated Press: 15, 17 (right), 28, 47, 48, 51, 54, 55, 57, 62, 63, 65, 71, 83, 96, 100, 126, 131, 145, 156, 165 (2), 168 (2), 169 (top), 172, 173 (bottom), 188 (2), 189, 190

AP/Corbis: 74

AP/Office of Independent Counsel: 133

Bettmann Archive/Corbis: 37, 39

Central Arkansas Library System, Bill Clinton State Government Project, Butler Center for Arkansas Studies: 34

Clinton Family Historical Collection, courtesy of the William J. Clinton Presidential Library: 3, 11 (top left and bottom right), 12 (left), 17 (left), 19, 23 (top), 27 (right), 31, 32–33, 36, 41

CNP/Corbis: 14

Corbis: 30, 68 (top), 72, 157 (top), 184 (bottom), 220, 221

FilmMagic/Getty: 211

Getty Images: 182 (bottom), 183, 193 (top), 195, 196, 197, 210, 212, 213 (2), 214 (bottom), 216, 217, 218 and 219 (2)

New York Daily News via Getty Images: 203, 215

Reuters/Corbis: 70, 82, 191, 201

Robert McNeely Photography: 60–61, 132 (top), 144 (bottom), 154, 158, 159

Shutterstock/mistydawnphoto: 214 (top)

Sygma/Corbis: 6 (right), 8 (left), 10, 11 (top right and bottom left), 13 (2), 18 (top), 22 (2), 23 (bottom), 24 (top right, bottom left, and bottom right), 26, 27 (left), 35, 38, 40, 42, 43, 45, 46, 49, 50, 52, 53, 56, 66, 67, 81, 90–91

Time-Life Pictures/Getty Images: 24 (top left), 25, 58–59, 64, 80, 134, 182

University of Arkansas Special Collections: 29

VII/Corbis: 69

Washington Times via Newsmakers/ Getty Images: 192 (bottom)

White House/Getty Images: 218

Wikimedia Commons: 18 (bottom)

Courtesy of the William J. Clinton Presidential Library: 6 (left), 7, 8 (right), 9, 12 (right), 20, 68 (bottom), 84, 85, 86–87, 88–89, 92, 93, 94, 95, 97, 98–99, 101 (2), 102, 103, 104, 105, 106–107, 108, 109, 110, 111, 112, 113 (2), 114–115, 116 (2), 117, 118, 119, 120, 121, 122, 123, 124, 125, 127, 128, 129, 132 (bottom), 135, 136, 137, 138, 142, 143, 144 (top), 152–153, 155, 157 (bottom), 160, 161, 162, 163 (2), 166–167, 169 (bottom), 170, 171, 174, 175 (2), 176, 177 (2), 178, 179, 180, 181 (2), 184 (top), 185, 186–187, 194, 198, 199, 200, 204, 205, 206, 207, 208, 209

CONTRIBUTORS

Created by David Elliot Cohen

Text by David Elliot Cohen and Curt Sanburn

Foreword by Chris Matthews

Design by Peter Truskier and David Elliot Cohen

Page production and image processing by Peter Truskier, Premedia Systems, Inc.

Photo research by Gina Privitere

Copy editing by Sherri Schultz

Proofreading by Sharon Vonasch

THANKS TO:

Central Arkansas Library System

Michael Fragnito, Barbara Berger, Elizabeth Mihaltse, Laura Healy, and Gillian Berman of Sterling Publishing

Josh Haner

John Keller and Herbert Ragan of the William J. Clinton Presidential Library and Museum

Bailey Noland of the Clinton Foundation

Eric Thayer

Tina Urbanski of *Hardball with Chris Matthews*

Glenn Whaley of the Bill Clinton State Government Project, Butler Center for Arkansas Studies